Making More Money for YOU!

Decrypting Cryptocurrency Riding the Data Path to Financial Freedom

By Magnus Carter

Please consult a licensed professional before attempting any techniques outlined in this book.

By reading this document, the reader agrees that under no circumstances is the author responsible for any losses, direct or indirect, which are incurred as a result of the use of the information contained within this document, including, but not limited to, — errors, omissions, or inaccuracies.

Table of Contents

Table of Contents

Introduction

You turn on the news after coming home from work, and the first story you see fills you up with rage. It is about how a teenage boy has just become a millionaire by investing in Bitcoin five years ago. A cascade of angry comments fog your mind, and you become irritated. Why is that your reaction instead of being happy for the boy? It is because you work tirelessly every day in a job that drains your soul to make just a few bucks, and some people get rich just by being lucky. A "JOB" might as well be an acronym for "Just Over Broke."

Who wouldn't be angry in this situation? Your success and ability to do things that you want all depend on how much money you have. Face it! You do not like working for your boss who cuts your salary when you take one day off. You do not want to be constantly nagged about a mistake made three weeks ago, nor do you want to sit in your office chair for 9 hours, which gives you cramps and back pain. The reason why you put up with them is that you need money to survive. How about I tell you that there are other ways to make money that doesn't require daily effort and humiliation. Just by being curious, having an open mind, and taking small risks, you can increase your wealth and be able to reach your financial goals in less time than you imagine. By following the path of self-learning, you will be on your way to a life in which you will never have to work again.

Maybe that boy was lucky, but luck is no longer the only way to take advantage of the rise of Bitcoin or Ethereum. Thousands of people, including billionaires and Wall Street giants, are investing in them right now and are gaining significant profits, more than you can ever imagine. It is estimated that the cryptocurrency market is going to reach a value of "1 trillion" this year. Suppose your dream is to become financially independent as soon as possible and want to retire early. In that case, you will need to convert this rage into curiosity and learn about investing, especially investing in one of the biggest growing commodities, which is cryptocurrency.

Cryptocurrency is a simple but new and tech-savvy idea which not many people understand. People investing in it sometimes have no clue about the risks and benefits associated with it and just participate because it has been trending on social media platforms. Like any other investment, it has its risks and benefits that you need to learn about. There are different types and methods to start your journey in this industry, and it all will depend on your financial situation and ability to handle risks. If many people do not understand the concept, even few can teach and advise newcomers to this market. If you want a complete guide with no-nonsense jargon and straightforward tips and tricks, then this book will be the best purchase you have ever made.

You might be wondering whether I can teach you? My name is Magnus Carter, a financially independent man supporting his entire family and also living his dreams. I was born in the heart of New York City to my parents that worked normal jobs and faced many financial difficulties in life. There were times in my home that made me question the way parents were living. They were both working, good people, but still, they struggled for necessities. So I started to explore new ways of earning money at an early age. Nobody taught me anything about investing, but by getting started, I gained lots of experience, and after two decades, I became the person I am today. I had made many mistakes, but by trying, I also made plenty of good decisions. My goal is to teach everyone how to improve their lives and escape financial stress and the rat race and make them able to pursue their goals.

Many people think that they had lost the chance of being successful when they were young, and now their fate is forever sealed. You might be one of those people that regret their lives and reminisce, constantly saying, "I could have done this, or I should have done that." The past is in the past, and you cannot change it, no matter how much you think about it. The past is fixed, but not your present state, nor your future. As long as you have a healthy body and a healthy mind, you can do anything and even change your living situation. You just need the determination to keep improving your life. You can do that by learning new skills and increasing your knowledge, and putting all these skills and knowledge into practice. You keep on practicing until one day, lady luck meets you. That is the day when you will laugh at your past.

If you do not follow the instructions in this book and procrastinate on the idea, then I am afraid you will have to keep working hard for money. Many people have dreams, but you can only achieve them if you make an effort towards them. Being a curious mind and increasing your knowledge of different opportunities have only helped people stay out of mediocrity. Putting all the information and knowledge into practice is the only way you will get to live the life you want. Therefore, you have to use all the information in this book to your advantage so that it increases the chances of your dreams coming true.

Not only will I show all the different options of cryptocurrency types, the most popular being Bitcoin, but also show you the inner workings and tell you how it works. You will be able to identify fraud and recognize top-performing currency to invest in. Big words like "Blockchain" and "Cryptography" will not confuse you anymore, but most importantly, I will tell you how to invest in them according to your lifestyle and preferences. You will explore all facets of this brave new world, from getting the right tools to the laws affecting the industry. All you have to do is to keep on reading.

Chapter 1: Where Did It Come From, Why Is It Here?

Everywhere you turn, you hear it. On the T.V, on radio, text messages, and advertisements. These news and events might have given you an idea of cryptocurrency. You know it is a type of electronic money, but that is where most people's understanding ends, and honestly, that is where my knowledge ended as well. We are going to explore the entire story of cryptocurrency together, so your understanding becomes as deep as the ocean.

The Decline of Physical Money

People around the world have started to transition towards electronic money for various reasons. You can live your life comfortably without carrying any physical cash. Physical money, when stolen, will not return to you. With extreme convenience and companies strengthening their security systems, the role of paper money is diminishing. Electronic money is more secure because it cannot be misplaced and has more transparency. It is accepted in multiple shops and even gas stations. You can find a card reader even in remote areas. In the U.S especially, there is a thorough and robust electronic money processing, which is facilitated through Visas and Mastercard. Banks and other financial institutions work with electronic money networks to provide more services to their customers. They issue cards and secure bank money transfers. Electronic money has given rise to e-commerce, and you can buy anything you want online from the comfort of your home.

You can put money in your account by direct deposit, transfer money using banking apps/websites, and purchase items using your debit and credit cards. However, with electronic money, you have to take your credit card with you, and if they get stolen, your card might get canceled. There is a limit on credit card use as well. When going to buy something, you also have to make sure if that place accepts cards or not. The rise of electronic money can increase the risk of fraud as well. Because credit card activities are recorded in banking data, they can monitor your purchasing patterns, look for irregularities, and minister overspending. They can sell this information to big companies that would target you for your buying behavior.

Electronic Money – The Predecessor to Cryptocurrency

Electronic money, like your money in savings and checking accounts, is stored in the banking computer system, and they are used for electronic money transfers. With the rise of the internet and websites like Amazon and eBay, electronic money has become more convenient, and sometimes it is the only currency they will accept. The process is handled through electronic processing, so many people consider it safer as well. In addition, it is interchangeable with fiat currency, so you can get traditional, physical notes in your hand by exchanging them. Fiat currency is backed by the government, and you can physically use them. Companies that work with this concept are brokers or middlemen. PayPal and Square are a few examples of them, and they allow customers to deposit and withdraw money. However, they charge a fee depending on how much money you are depositing, transferring, or withdrawing, so you need to first check with them to find out their rate.

Fact

Fiat Money is a currency backed by the government and does not change when the price of commodities changes, such as gold, silver, bronze, oil, and other valuable resources. The central banks control the currency by maintaining a steady money supply. An example of fiat currency is paper money such as the U.S. dollar.

The Beginning of Cryptocurrencies

Around the time DigiCash was on the market, many people started to further the idea of secure money transfers through the internet. One of them was the now successful company, PayPal. They revolutionized web-based money transfers by linking themselves to a dedicated community of eBay and continuing to grow and upgrade their technology. The company had many imitators, and a new line array of companies dabbling in digital currencies sprung. One of them was e-gold. With e-gold, you would get credit in exchange for gold and other expensive metals. Unfortunately, they were forced to shut down in 2005 due to increased cases of money laundering.

Fact

By 2004, e-gold had 2 million users, and by 2006, it counted for 3 billion transactions. Because of the high percentage of criminals using the system, the U.S. Treasury and Justice Department put strict laws and then filed e-gold with federal charges.

In the late 90s, a developer named Wei Da conceptualized B-money, which was a secure, anonymous electronic cash. It was never launched officially but introduced the concept in 1998, in a published essay. The system worked on two protocols, and one of them needed a synchronized, unjammable broadcast channel. It worked very differently than bitcoin today, but it was an attempt at a digital currency, which transferred money through a decentralized network. When bitcoin issued their whitepaper, they mentioned B-money, so they have left an impact on the cryptocurrency world.

Fact

A whitepaper is a document released by an organization that shows their services to solve a problem, offers, and is used to promote their company or a product.

In the early 2000s, when B-money was around, another cryptocurrency was introduced called Bit Gold. Introduced by Nick Szabo, it was an attempt to mimic the decentralized nature of gold and remove the requirement of a middle man entirely.

Among all the earliest digital currencies, the most successful bitcoin predecessor was HashCash. It was launched in the mid-90s and had relatively good security to stop many potential hackers and identify spam. It was made to maintain the steady generation and distribution of the currency. Unfortunately, the concept was too soon for its time, as the project collapsed due to a lack of technology available.

You may only know of bitcoin, but today's age of digital currency is built upon the foundation work of these attempts at cryptocurrencies. Bitcoin took inspiration from many of these companies and made an effort to remove the commonly seen mistakes.

Many people assume that Bitcoin was the first cryptocurrency ever made, but that is false. Nowadays, the investing sites and markets are filled with all kinds of cryptocurrencies and their apps, but the most dominant of them all is still Bitcoin. The trends and fame of digital currency indeed started with its success, but many have come before it.

One of the earliest attempts ever recorded was in the Netherlands in the 90s. The gas stations were frequently being attacked by thieves, and it was dangerous to hold physical money. So instead of placing guards, a few developers designed new smart cards that would allow people to access the stations and remove the need for physical money.

Also, in the 90s, an American cryptographer named David Chaum played with the idea of electronic cash and developed a program for it. He introduced a token (do not worry, this will be covered in the next chapter) that could be safely and privately transferred between individuals, just like modern-day cryptocurrencies. The token would be encrypted using David's "blinding formula." The system would require specific encrypted keys before the money could be transferred. These blind signatures improved its security. The token would have authenticity and be decrypted without traceability. David Chaum started his company "DigiCash" with this concept. The company went bankrupt, but the method used to make DigiCash is similar to how people make digital currencies today.

Fact

Cryptography is a study of secure communication techniques. Secure communication means that only the sender and recipient of the message will be able to see its contents. A person who develops such techniques is a cryptographer.

What Is Cryptocurrency?

Now, you know that bitcoin and other cryptocurrencies are entering the lives of the general public, and their existence is appreciated and accepted by millions of individual customers worldwide, so many that big governments are now forming laws around it.

Cryptocurrency is a method of exchanging value in a unit of measure. It is made up of nothing more than code and, individually, has no value. However, the value is added when cryptocurrency is used to price other commodities. For example, when bitcoin was launched in 2009, it was a means of payment, but it was only worth how much it was being traded for. Bitcoins are digital assets or crypto assets, and their value is shown by the effectiveness of their cryptography and blockchain. The original intent of these assets is to become a method of transferring value without third-party members. There are three main types of digital or crypto assets:

- Cryptocurrencies like Bitcoin
- Crypto commodities
- Crypto tokens

Fact

In cryptocurrency, the most important features of cryptography being used are Hashing and Digital Signatures. Hashing checks the data integrity, holds the blockchain together, and encrypts data like addresses and transactions. Digital signatures prove that a certain transaction belongs to an individual without showing the encrypted data. It works as a sign that proves authenticity.

One of the important features of cryptocurrencies is that they are designed to reduce production when time passes. They will work like commodities such as gold and precious metals. Only a limited number of units or coins of a cryptocurrency will be in circulation. This is how bitcoin works. Ethereum, however, takes a slightly different approach. Per year, there is a cap or a limit of how many tokens are introduced. Bitcoin mimicking precious metals makes its value rise as the more scarce the bitcoin gets.

Cryptocurrency is different from electronic money because it is not interchangeable with fiat currency and is not backed by the government. That is why it is referred to as "decentralized." It has no central body governing laws around it. Moreover, cryptocurrencies only live in cyberspace or the internet. As a result, they are untraceable, unlike electronic money, and no third party will charge an extra fee for deposits, withdrawals, and transfers.

Fact

An organization's activities most of the time are controlled by a central, authoritative group or location. In cryptocurrency, the process of planning and decision-making is distributed. That is why it is referred to as decentralized.

The Birth of Bitcoin

In 2009, an unknown programmer, or programmers, working under the pseudonym Satoshi Nakamoto, developed bitcoin. Satoshi then published his Bitcoin whitepaper, which had details of how bitcoin and blockchain worked.

A few months later, Mr. Satoshi mined the Genesis Block(discussed later). It was the first block of the Bitcoin system. This gave a blueprint of blockchain technology to the world. This is where the term blockchain comes from. The first purchase from Bitcoin was made by Florida man Laszlo Hanyecz. He purchased two pizzas by using bitcoin, and this date is known as 'Bitcoin Pizza Day' and comes every year on May 22.

Fact

When some transaction data is stored, it is made up in the form of a list. This is known as one block. A chain is made when a series of stacks of blocks are added on top of each other, which grows over time. It is extremely hard to change this information when a block or data set is deep in history or far away from the chain's end. This makes it great for storing data.

Fact

The original Genesis block is the base of the chain, the first transaction data in Blockchain technology.

Bitcoin started to gain a little traction, and in March 2010, the world's first cryptocurrencies exchange was launched. Later that year, Mt.Gox was open to the public as well.

Fact

The gaining popularity made bitcoin reach the value of the U.S dollar in 2013.

Other cryptocurrencies started to gain attention in the market as well, such as Litecoin and XRP. During the emergence of rival currencies and copycats, bitcoin was criticized on the media and social media for providing a source of the transaction on the "dark web," which hosts sites such as Silk Road. However, the criticisms increased the general awareness of bitcoin which led to the rise in the price of BTCs (bitcoins).

Fact

The dark web is a hidden section of the internet that hosts multiple websites that can only be seen by a specialized browser. These websites mostly deal with illegal activities, but because of all higher levels of privacy and anonymity, it is useful in many legal activities as well.

At this time, the popularity of bitcoin reached the parliament of some countries, with Thailand and China banning cryptocurrency transactions altogether. A massive drop in bitcoins value was seen after these announcements. In addition, Germany refused to recognize bitcoin as an official currency but gave it a status of "unit of account." This could lead to bitcoin being taxed in the future.

This year, Microsoft allowed its users to use bitcoin to buy games.

2016 was a major year for bitcoin, as cryptocurrency was becoming more mainstream and accepted in the public eye. As a result, Bitcoin ATMs started to pop up in areas, and almost 500 ATMs were opened in one year. In addition, major companies like Uber allowed their customers in Argentina to use bitcoins as a method of payment. The Swiss national railway and Steam (an online game store) were other places where bitcoin would be accepted were the Swiss national railway and Steam (which is an online game store).

In 2017, a bitcoin fork occurred, which split the currency into two, BTC and bitcoin cash. The Japanese government passed a law that allowed bitcoin to be used as a legal form of payment. Also, a city in Norway started to accept bitcoin as a legal form of investment and payment system.

After a year, in 2018, Samsung got interested in bitcoins as well and stated that they were making chips to mine bitcoin. The European government together cooperated to make laws for cryptocurrency regulations.

Bitcoin's value has been growing ever since, and more and more people are taking an interest in it.

The Second Largest Cryptocurrency: Ethereum

In the middle of 2015, the new cryptocurrency, Ethereum, was made public. This cryptocurrency had a different approach than bitcoin in transferring money. Ethereum introduced the concept of smart contracts into the cryptocurrency market. A "smart contract" is nothing but a set of functions that make the transaction safe without the need of a third party. It is like any other security software. Putting this function in their transfer service allowed Ethereum blockchain to run fully on its ecosystem. Ether (ETH) is the native currency of Ethereum.

Blockchains are required for cryptocurrency to work, but not every digital currency has them. The currencies that use other crypto asset's blockchains are known as tokens. Many use the Ethereum blockchain; these currencies are called ERC-20 tokens. The first-ever token and ERC-20 token was launched in 2015, called Augur. Ethereum blockchain hosts about 200,000 tokens, which makes it the largest ecosystem for cryptocurrency transactions.

The Situation Today

The cryptocurrency world has been rising more than ever. The prices are reaching all-time highs and breaking their records after a few months. A lot of other crypto assets have joined the market and are gaining traction; some of them are:

- EOS launched in July 2017

- Tron launched in September 2017

- Cardano launched in October 2017

It is shocking to believe that the industry could grow at a pace like a cryptocurrency. Just five years ago, a BTC's value was less than 1000 dollars. The prices are going through the roof, and it is still expanding at a massive rate. More and more shops have adopted a crypto-friendly environment, and Bitcoin ATMs are being opened up around the country. You can order your food, start a fundraiser or even travel the world on the only cryptocurrency.

More expansion plans are in process to make the market more global. Its popularity and wide range of acceptance have fueled the creation of CBDC, Central Bank Digital Currency. A lot of big companies are showing an interest in cryptocurrency and are willing to invest in it. A great expansion is yet to come.

Fact

A public blockchain is a distributed ledger, which acts as a database and has specific features. The most important features are: that it is decentralized, it is distributed across the entire global network, it is encrypted, anonymous, and cannot change the data once it is entered into the ledger.

Why Is Cryptocurrency So Popular?

There are multiple reasons for its popularity and why it is spreading fast. Cryptocurrency comes with a lot of features that were not available previously to anyone with paper or electronic money.

Privacy

The key feature is privacy when it comes to cryptocurrency. The receiver, on the other side, will get their money without unnecessary information needed in between. This means that your private information and financial statements will be protected by banks, advertisers, payment services, and credit card agencies. In addition, because there is no sensitive or confidential information being sent, the information being compromised is highly unlikely.

Portability

You can access your cryptocurrency holdings and use them anywhere in the world. When using a bank, there can be problems as each bank has to follow their home country's laws, which sometimes makes processing tiring and difficult. Problems can arise when you need to access the money immediately. The global financial system and country policies will not affect your life and your holdings.

Transparency

When a transaction is completed using cryptocurrency like Ethereum, bitcoin, bitcoin cash, etc., it is made public immediately. Thus, there is no time between the transaction, and it becomes public for anyone, be it an inside person or hacker, to manipulate and change the money supply or the rules.

Irreversibility

It is extremely jarring to see credit card charges added to the price when purchasing anything online. Unlike card payments, the transaction cannot be reversed. The vendors and suppliers can benefit from this as it is less likely to get defrauded using this system. For consumers, the price of e-commerce and products online will become cheaper.

Safety

The fundamental ideas behind cryptocurrency help make the network powering safe and it's never been hacked. For computer scientists and cryptographers, it's easy to examine all aspects of the networks and their security because the system is permissionless and the core software is open-source.

Chapter 2: Why Are There So Many Different Types?!?!

Before 2010, the cryptocurrency world was empty. Digital currencies were a new concept, and it needed time for word to spread and support to gather; fortunately, it did not take long. After bitcoin was launched and success was seen with it, other developers started to adopt the blockchain technology and make their cryptocurrencies and tokens. People saw this as an opportunity to create something that can grow as fast as bitcoin in the market and create good business for themselves. So many types and kinds of crypto have been introduced since then, all with great potential. As bitcoin gets popular, so do other cryptocurrencies. There are over 10,000 different types in circulation, and the race for making more is not slowing down. The market capitalization is estimated to be around 2 trillion.

Types of Cryptocurrencies

The different types of cryptocurrencies all are based on the same principle, such as being decentralized and encrypted. Still, each type offers some new functions or features that you cannot find in others.

Generally, cryptocurrency has two distinct forms. These are:

- Coins: This includes bitcoin and altcoins.
- Tokens: assets that are made in a pre-existing blockchain platform.

What Are Tokens?

Generally, tokens are round pieces of plastic or metal that look like a coin and can be used on different machines that allow it, for example arcade machines in gaming centers. They are a representation of a real coin and work as a real coin, but only in certain places. This is true with crypto tokens as well. A token is a representation of cryptocurrencies that can be used only in specific areas.

Tokens are transferred through a system similar to a stock exchange. It is called an ICO or Initial Coin Offering.

They are categorized into 3 main types:

- Value tokens
- Security tokens
- Utility tokens

Fact

Value tokens work as bitcoins, while security tokens work like stocks. Utility tokens are assigned to assets and are used in specific situations. They are not valuable themselves, just like a dollar paper is not worth one dollar, but the value is assigned to them. They are used during transactions of other assets.

How Tokens Are Different from Coins?

Many people working with crypto use tokens and coins interchangeably, but there are significant differences between them.

Coins are made in their blockchain, and they are meant to be traded as a currency. Bitcoin (BTC) is based on the bitcoin blockchain and Ethereum (ETH) on the Ethereum blockchain. Cryptocurrencies that have their blockchain and are not bitcoin are called altcoins. Tokens are different because they are not meant to be traded as currencies. They are made in an existing blockchain but are programmed assets that people use to create smart contracts. These contracts can determine whether a person owns an asset or not, even outside the blockchain it works on. They are linked with value and can be used to assign this value to digital and real-world items, for example, electricity, money, or digital assets. They can effectively be transferred between two parties. One of the most popular tokens on the Ethereum blockchain is BAT or Basic Attention Token.

This token is primarily used for assigning value in digital advertising.

Alternative Cryptocurrency Coins or Altcoins

Altcoins is an abbreviation or shorthand term for "alternative to bitcoin." Any coin that is not bitcoin is known as an altcoin. Most altcoins were introduced to overcome the shortcomings of bitcoin. Many Altcoins have a limited supply of their coins so that it grows in demand and value, just like bitcoin. Bitcoin and other altcoins share fundamental principles of cryptocurrencies, but each performs a specific function different from the others, either to make it better or to fit a certain situation. For instance, Litecoin has lower fees than bitcoin, but both are cryptocurrencies that run on blockchain technology. Some have low price volatility, and some have different methods to check block transactions.

There are thousands of altcoins today, but the first altcoin produced was Namecoin in 2011. Some other examples of altcoins include:

- Peercoin
- Litecoin
- Dogecoin
- Auroracoin

Bitcoin is an open-source system, and many altcoins run on separate systems that are not open source. Altcoins with their own blockchain are proprietary to the makers of blockchain. They have their features, protocols and support their coins. These include:

- Ethereum
- Litecoin
- Ripple
- Stellar, etc.

The Popular Cryptocurrencies of The World

With thousands of cryptocurrencies out there, some have made a great change and provided game-changing features. As a result, they have become one of the biggest names in cryptocurrencies, and their market capitalization is rising. Because there are so many virtual currencies, the market value helps determine which ones are of most value.

1. Bitcoin

The name "Bitcoin" is synonymous with big brand names like "Coca Cola" or "Kleenex" because it is the first thing people think of when someone mentions crypto. The popularity and history of cryptocurrencies started with the success of Bitcoin, and its creation inspired others to join in. It is most associated with the cryptocurrency system, as cryptography helps maintain and generate Bitcoins. Bitcoin has a limit amount of 21 million, 18 million of which are in circulation.

It is designed to make banking systems and any government interaction and influence on our money to become obsolete. Its blockchain technology works as a ledger of all bitcoin transfers. Bitcoin forms the basis of digital currencies and cryptography, which is the foundation of cryptocurrencies.

Miners of bitcoin use powerful computers to check transaction blocks to make new coins for themselves. It is an extremely complex and time-consuming work termed as (PoW) or Proof of Work. The energy required is so high that people have started commenting on its effect on pollution.

2. Bitcoin Cash

The second biggest fork in the bitcoin world divided bitcoin into two, bitcoin and bitcoin cash. Launched in 2017, bitcoin cash is one of the most popular cryptocurrencies. The difference between bitcoin and bitcoin cash is its block size. A Bitcoin's original block size is 1M.B., but a Bitcoin Cash's block size is 8MB. Programmers found a loophole that would help transactions be faster and have more bit size on the current system. It is similar to when coca cola came up with a new formula under the same brand name later on after the brand name was already established. This makes for a better user experience because the system has faster processing speeds.

3. Litecoin

It is one of the earliest altcoins launched, being introduced in 2011 by Charlie Lee. He was a former Google employee and made Litecoin improve on the technology of bitcoin. It is used similarly to bitcoin but with additional features. And, transaction times are shorter, and they require fewer fees for different purposes. There are also more concentrated miners in Litecoin.

4. Ethereum

It is mainly a blockchain platform rather than to be used as a generalized digital currency. It is a blockchain network that is programmable, so it was not meant to support a currency. Instead, it was meant to help network users to create, publish and make money off of applications, known as "dapps." In September 2021, Ether became the second most successful coin after bitcoin.

It focuses more on making decentralized apps for phones. It can be looked at as an app store rather than a direct competition of bitcoin. Ethereum's idea is to take control away from the middleman of apps, like Apple, and give the original markers of the app the power to change and control it. There will be no money wasted between the buyer and the purchaser of the app. It hosts a multitude of tokens as well called Ether. They are used as currency in Ethereum's platform.

Ethereum's platform has birthed many initial coin offerings and increased the popularity of different digital assets such as NFTs, Non-fungible tokens.

Fact

NFTs are digital versions of artworks that are programmed to be unique and used in an exciting blockchain.

5. Ripple or XRP

XRP was launched by Ripple Lab, Inc. Ripple and XRP are used interchangeably, but they represent two different aspects. Ripple is a global money transferring company used by financial service networks. At the same time, XRP is a cryptocurrency made to be used in the Ripple network. XRP is kind of an exception. Even though it is a type of cryptocurrency, it does not follow blockchain-based programming.

As a member of the general public, you cannot work with XRP. It is meant only for large money transfers between corporations and companies. XRP is the coinage system for Ripple, which is more famous for its digital payment protocol than the coin. It can transfer all kinds of currency, whether bitcoin or U.S. dollars. It can also handle 1,500 transactions per second (TPS). Bitcoin can only handle a maximum of 6tps and Ethereum 15tps.

XRP, unlike bitcoin, cannot be mined, and there is a limited number of them in circulation, 100 billion. XRP also does not use the digital verification procedure that bitcoin and other altcoins have. Instead, it uses the Ripple network to validate transactions. That is why XRP's transactions are faster and cheaper.

Fact

Scaling is the limit to which a cryptocurrency's blockchain processes transactions. To overcome this setback, Cryptocurrencies have scaling layers. Layer 1 is blockchain processing, and level 2 is the integration of third parties to work alongside layer 1.

6. Stellar

Stellar was launched in 2014 by the co-founder of Ripple, Jed McCaleb. This coin is run by the non-profit organization Stellar.org. The coin focuses on money transfers across nations being more effective and fast.

The main idea of Stellar is to help developing economies by giving them an option of transferring money without banks and the governmental influence of their country, which may not have their best interest. People that do not have access to good quality banks and investment opportunities use this coin. The Stellar network being a non-profit, does not charge users or organizations any fee for using its network. It covers its operating fees by accepting donations from around the world.

7. NEO

Neo is an open-source cryptocurrency platform that is rivaling Ethereum. It was known as Antshares and was launched in China. Advertisements and upgrades have been pushing Neo to become one of the highest global cryptocurrencies. Just like Ethereum, Neo focuses more on smart contracts or digital contracts. This helps users to make agreements without needing a third party.

The main developer of Neo, Erik Zhang, once posted how this new platform is better than others that came before it. Ethereum claims to create a platform where anybody can create apps and control them, but they first have to learn Ethereum's unique programming to do it. Developers need to learn a different language to work on the platform. However, Neo is different. It has three main benefits, which are

- Better architecture
- Developer friendly
- Easy integration of digital assets in the real world

8. Cardano Or ADA

The co-founder of Ethereum, Charles Hoskinson, launched Cardano as third-generation blockchain technology. It works on a different principle than bitcoin. Rather than relying on PoW, which consumes lots of energy and complex mathematical solving codes, it uses PoS (Power of Stake). This eliminates pollution and electricity wastage and makes its platform more efficient and sustainable.

Cardano is a blockchain platform with ADA as its cryptocurrency and is named after 19th-century mathematician Ada Lovelace. Cardano shares its scientific philosophy and research-driven approach to other scientific fields. Its roadmap is constantly investigated, and upgrades are supported by peer-reviewed insights and frameworks. Because of this, Cardano has received a scholarly reputation.

Cardano mainly is used to transferring digital funds, focusing mostly on traceability and management. It can trace and streamline multiple data coming from multiple sources. This ensures that the product's entire path is recorded and there is less chance of fraud.

The development of Cardano will take five phases in which, in the end, the network will become decentralized, host applications or "dapps" and smart contracts with a multi-asset ledger.

9. IOTA

The platform IOTA and its cryptocurrency MIOTA is a distributed, open-source, free-to-use ledger that stands for Internet of Things Application. It is used to record and execute transfers between devices in the IOTA ecosystem. This cryptocurrency does not use blockchain technology but instead uses Tangle. Tangle is a system of nodes by which MIOTA checks its transactions. This method is more efficient and faster than typical blockchain processing. To use IOTA, you need to first check two previous transactions. Using it, a device can buy more data, bandwidth, storage, etc., when they need them and sell them when they do not need them.

Today, devices from phones to cars to smart fridges all are connected by the internet. This (IoT) Internet of things ecosystem allows information to be transferred between them. Using this cryptocurrency, we will be able to get transactions between devices, and anyone can access it.

10. USD Coin (USDC)

This is a type of stable coin (discussed later) that works within different blockchain platforms, including Ethereum. The USDC coin is pegged with the U.S. dollar, meaning one USDC is worth one U.S. dollar. This is a guaranteed ratio. This makes the transaction of money cheaper and faster, and it is more transparent. As of June 2021, there were 24.1 billion USDC in use.

These cryptocurrencies are made to improve upon blockchain technology, provide more features and a more diverse range of applications. They, together, are taking part in revolutionizing finance and other aspects of society linked with it. Social networking, data storage, privacy, security, payments, and machine learning, etc., are all being upgraded with the advancement of crypto.

Thousands of Cryptocurrencies, But Why?

There are many reasons why cryptocurrencies are as big as they are today.

- **Open-Source**

Cryptocurrencies are backed by blockchain technology. This technology is open-source, allowing computer scientists and developers to create new cryptocurrencies with the original code. Hundreds of people have done just that. Developers add new functions to each crypto so that it improves on one or two aspects. As a result, the many cryptocurrencies each have unique functionalities.

- **Massive Profit**

When bitcoin was released in 2009, no one paid any attention to it. Even when it was starting to rise, the general behavior was to disregard and ignore it. However, the value was substantially appreciated in just a couple of years, bringing in lots of profit to people who first invested in them. Even Ethereum was worthless, and many people did not have any high expectations for it. Now, its value has been appreciated as well, racking in huge profits.

- **Forking**

Many big cryptocurrencies have, in their lifetime, split into two branches because of demand and disagreements, usually about the supply and transfer system. Bitcoin was split into bitcoin cash and bitcoin gold. It is responsible for a few new types of famous cryptocurrencies.

- **Innovation**

  When you open the App store on your phone, you look for an app with a particular purpose. In your search, you see hundreds of options to choose from. Each app provides a unique way of doing the task, even if it is the same task. Some have a great design, and some are minimalistic. Some focus on providing the most function, and some focus on providing the cheapest solution for the consumer. There is a kind for everyone.

  Cryptocurrencies are generated with the same thought. Developers are trying to improve the process by adding new features and experimenting with new ideas.

- **Stable Currency**

  Cryptocurrencies offer some great services, but the main disadvantage of them would be instability. It has only been a decade since their inception, and during this time, they have gained enough support from millions of people. However, it is not at a state of challenging real fiat currencies of countries right now. Therefore, for crypto to gain more stability, stable coins were introduced.

In our list, the USD coin is a prime example of a stable coin. You can imagine them to be dollars in crypto form, taking advantage of utility and services while minimizing uncertainty and volatility. The features that make cryptocurrencies attractive, such as private global transactions, are enjoyed without risking the worth of that coin.

There are two ways stable coins do this, first, by backing themselves with a physical commodity like gold. Or secondly, backing themselves up with an established fiat currency.

Like any other traditional savings account, you can use them, depositing, withdrawing, and transferring money at a constant value. The setback is that the price of these coins will not decrease, but they will not increase in value either. One of the reasons cryptocurrencies are appealing is that they have proved to be one of the greatest investments of all time. To miss out on the opportunities provided by cryptocurrencies in our era would be a big mistake, so let's talk about how to begin investing in them.

Chapter 3: I Need More Tech! But What Tech Do I Need?

Like any other new device, Cryptocurrency and Blockchain follow a unique system that makes them able to complete their objective. With a system linked with money transfers, you should be extremely knowledgeable and careful when choosing which technology to invest in. It is quite nerve-wracking to put your hard-earned dollars into a plan that is relatively new to you. To become completely confident in your investment, firstly, you need to understand the technical side of cryptocurrency and how it works.

This technology requires adding new cryptocurrency into the system, efficiently and quickly transferring it along with the entire global network. And thus, satisfy the customer and deter hackers and thieves from stealing money or using the system for their gains. For this, much trial and error have gone through the last decade to ensure secure running blockchains.

Understanding Blockchain

To give you a refresher, Blockchain technology works by building up a chain of transaction information or "blocks." These blocks are created when time-stamped data is checked through a person's powerful computer, situated anywhere in the world. The checking process is called PoW (proof of work). This is also called a hash-based proof of work because they are hashed into the chain after checking the data. The data in the chain are treated as records and cannot be changed unless the person redoes the entire PoW program on the data. This data, however, is already deep inside the system and hard to retrieve.

When a fresh set of information is formed through a transaction, it is stored inside a new block. This block, once filled, is added to the block made just before it. This cycle continues, and the data blocks join together one by one, turning into a bigger chain. This chain is placed in chronological order, meaning according to the time. Thus, an old set of data will be below the chain, and new ones will be at the open end or the top. The data mostly used to make the blocks are of transaction ledgers, the information about transferring money, but they can store other types as well.

Most cryptocurrencies, as well as Bitcoin and Litecoin, blockchains are set up in a decentralized system. Every individual who has some Bitcoin or any cryptocurrency that follows this model has a tiny control over it. The entire control is collectively distributed to all users so that no single person or single group is changing the rules and having a great amount of power over other people's money.

Fact

The individual computers that come together and use the programming of Blockchain are called nodes.

The main reason for the emergence of cryptocurrency was security and privacy. Decentralized blockchains make it impossible to reverse or change the data. If you work at a bank, it is possible for someone working in the bank to change your data, the amount of money you possess, and they can leak your security details. It is extremely easy for them to steal your account balance as well. In cryptocurrency, there is no organization handling the processes, and the data entered is irreversible. This means that transaction records can be seen by everyone permanently and are safe from being changed.

Blockchains programming reassembles a database, where a computer or a program stores all its data, but it has its differences. It does not act like your typical database by just storing information. Instead, the data in Blockchains are chained together and stored in mini storage units called blocks. Each cryptocurrency has a different unit of a block, for example, 1MB for Bitcoin and 8MB for bit cash, which changes the user's experience. One block in Bitcoin can consist of data made up of 500 Bitcoin transactions.

For further understanding of blockchain workings, you need to be able to understand how databases handle storage. It may seem complicated, but after you have understood the core concept, you will know that it is a simple mechanic.

Database and Blockchain

The most important aspect of a Blockchain is data storage structure, which is also the main difference between it and a typical database. Information collected does not go directly inside the database but is made into a group called a block before it can be saved. This block is where the cryptocurrencies information is hiding. The storage capacity is different for every cryptocurrency. Still, when it is filled, it gets added to the previously formed block to make a regular chronological structure.

A typical database does not follow this routine. It sets the data into tables, and each data is not linked with one another in any form. It does not fit a group of similar or separate data into groups for storage or makes a block-like unit for them. A database can assign all sorts of perimeters to search data, for example, file size, file type, filename, etc. They spend a lot of time using sensitive information to access data as well. This does not happen in the Blockchain.

You can say that all blockchains are databases in that they store data, but not all databases are blockchains. There are many types of databases in the world but function differently to fit a specific purpose.

This structural difference makes the data add into an irreversible universe, where the timeline is set in stone and seen by everyone using this decentralized system. The data is only differentiated by the timestamps of the blocks. No other information, sensitive or insensitive, is attached to it.

Fact

Blockchains can also be referred to as "Distributed Ledger Technology" or DLT for short.

Blockchain Explorer

Blockchains are the base, the foundations of cryptocurrencies such as bitcoin, and their success is directly related to the effectiveness of their security. The use of Blockchain involves specialist tools for managing and viewing the assets being produced, transferred, and distributed. One software that helps in doing this is Blockchain explorer.

Using a blockchain, anyone can view transaction data, even though they cannot change it. A blockchain explorer works like a search engine to navigate data stored in the Blockchain. An example of it would be Bitcoin Blockchain explorer or BTC, and it helps people to see the wallet addresses and transaction details. A person can see these data from any computer.

The blockchain explorer uses a program that is called API or Application Programming Interface. This helps a node to bring information from the blockchain network. The software then arranges the data into a searchable format in a database and presents it in front of the user. Next, the explorer searches the database according to the input of the user. This functionality allows people to search data about mined blocks and recent transactions. Some software gives you a real-time feed of transactions and mining.

What can Blockchain Explorer do?

There are other functions that Blockchain explorers can perform; some of them are:

- Can tell you the details of transactions of specific wallets. This increases transparency and enables the public to perform audits.

Fact

An audit is an official financial inspection of companies or accounts. It is typically done by an independent individual.

- See wallet addresses that receive cryptocurrency and return tokens to anyone that spends cryptocurrency by changing addresses.
- Look at the unconfirmed transactions and their data by looking at their status.
- Find orphaned blocks. These blocks are not attached to the main Blockchain and whose parent blockchain is not found even after mining.
- Explore stale blocks whose parent chain is known but still are not attached to them.
- Some Blockchain Explorers have a feature in which a person can see the largest transactions of a particular day.
- Some explorers allow people to see how many double-spend transactions occur at a certain time.

Fact

Double spend transactions are potential flaws of the blockchain system in which a coin or token can be spent twice.

Popular Blockchain Explorers

Other than Blockchain explorer, there are other applications in cryptocurrency providing similar assistance. Blockchair is a search engine for Bitcoin cash and a few others. Tokenview is an explorer that runs on more than 20 blockchains. Etherscan is the most popular search engine in the Ethereum blockchain.

Blockchain technology has made sending money as easy as email. Before the internet, we had to pay providers to send messages, but after the advent of the internet, this has declined rapidly. Blockchain technology has made cryptocurrency move swiftly, like emails by cryptography and its unique protocols.

What is Protocol?

A protocol for Blockchain is a pre-established procedure or set of instructions that govern the entire system and processes of the application, given any circumstances. In the English language, it means to set rules for diplomatic affairs such as "the president shall not make any public statements" or "it is a protocol that the contents of the contract be read and accepted by both parties," etc.

Blockchain Properties

The two properties that make Blockchain what it is are

- Immutability
- Ability to be distributed

Immutability

This just means that you can be fully confident with the data. The information stored in the system is accurate and unable to change.

Distributed

This property allows any user to see the transaction data and is protected by network attackers, and any anomaly can be caught quickly.

Types of Blockchain

There are four types of Blockchain that cryptocurrency uses today and these are:

- Public Blockchain
- Private Blockchain

- Consortiums or Hybrid Blockchain
- Sidechains

Public Blockchain

These kinds of Blockchain are open-sourced and decentralized. Many computers connected to a network can request, see and validate a transaction. To validate a transaction means to check its accuracy. People who check (miners) receive coins and tokens as a reward for their work. They do this by using the PoW system or PoS system to check the blocks. The most popular Blockchain in the cryptocurrency world is Bitcoin and Ethereum blockchains.

Private Blockchains

These blockchains are not open-sourced, and they have restrictions on how many people can access the system. There is a systems administrator that you have to get permission from to fully utilize the blockchain functionalities. They have one administrator or a group of people that control the inner workings, which means they are centralized. An example of it would be Hyperlegder. It is a classic private blockchain.

Hybrid Blockchain or Consortiums

These blockchains have a set of protocols that resembles both a public blockchain and a private one. This means that they have centralized and also decentralized aspects. Some examples of hybrid Blockchain are Energy Web Foundation, Dragonchain, R3, etc.

Fact

Consortiums and Hybrid Blockchain are terms that are frequently said interchangeably. Still, many people argue that there is a difference between them. Both of these views are still being debated, evenly split between those who believe them to be the same and different.

Sidechains

This is a blockchain that runs alongside or simultaneously with the main Blockchain. If you can move data between the two blockchains, then the digital assets are safer. This method improves scalability and efficiency. A liquid network is one such example of a sidechain.

The First Blockchain

The protocols that make blockchain work were first laid down by a cryptographer named David Chaum in the early 1980s. Later on, other computer scientists, Stuart Haber and W. Scott Stornetta, wrote a paper explaining how a Consortium would work. This was done in the early 1990s.

The mysterious group that made Bitcoin and who is hiding behind Satoshi Nakamoto's name is the first person to have implemented and made a working blockchain system. With this new invention of his, he gave the world its first digital currency, Bitcoin. There have been advances, and newly upgraded blockchains have been released since then.

Block Mining

It is a process by which new units are made and added to the circulation. It has an effect similar to mining rare metals. Taking an example of bitcoin, when new transaction records are added as blocks, new bitcoins are produced. You can find these coins by making a specific software that solves mathematical puzzles and validates the transaction. When a software successfully mines or validates a block, the miner gets a reward of bitcoins.

This is why the unit does not require a central system. Instead, these miners or volunteers can validate the data from anywhere in the world.

Inner Workings of a Public Blockchain – A Step by step guide

A ledger is a document that stores information and can be used in many areas. For example, there are ledgers stating house records for the real estate industry and have information on them, such as the original price of the house and the renovations done. Ledgers are mainly used to describe financial records or bookkeeping of a company showing their transaction details and accounting numbers. Bookkeeping is maintained through double-entry accounting mainly. The sender and the receiver both have a record of a specific transaction. This greatly increases the transparency and accountability of the transaction and is an upgrade from a single entry. However, it has its disadvantages.

Firstly, each entry is going to be written separately; one is with the receiver and one with the seller. This makes it difficult to check the other party's entry and verify each other's records. Secondly, if you have typed in a spreadsheet or handwritten the data, it can be easily tampered with. Anyone that has access to the records can edit the contents by removing, adding, and changing the numbers involved. This makes the double-entry system less trustworthy because you are never sure if the information is accurate or not.

Public Blockchains are also a type of ledger. It is a ledger of transactions on the internet, but this system solves both the problems described above. Blockchain technology takes one step further, and rather than doing the typical double entry, it does triple entry bookkeeping. The third entry is sealed, cryptographically, as a "block" in the ever-expanding Blockchain.

The third entry makes an unchangeable record of the transaction, and the data is then checked by a distributed mechanism. This is called a consensus mechanism, and helps get new blocks added to the pre-existing Blockchain. An example of a consensus mechanism would be PoW or the act of Mining.

Bitcoin adds new coins to the system through mining, but it is not the only system out there. It is just one type of many consensus mechanisms. Ethereum also uses this type of consensus but has decided to change it to another type called PoS by 2022.

How Does Bitcoin Work?

It is very simple to understand the workings of Bitcoin. When you are sending Bitcoin to someone else, a little bit of your bitcoin goes to pay a small fee. This is for a network to check your transaction. When you have made a recent transaction, then it is queued behind other transactions waiting to get added to a block.

An individual volunteer using a node (computer) then uses their device to check all the transactions saved inside the block. This is done by solving complicated mathematical problems that, in the end, come up with a Hash. A hash is a 64-digit hexadecimal number.

When the nodes have solved or checked the blocks, they are added to the main Blockchain. Your fee of bitcoins goes to the volunteer/miner as a reward for checking the data.

Cryptocurrencies Wallets

Cryptocurrencies wallets are important to have when buying any kind of cryptocurrency. They save your private keys that encrypt your transfer and currency amount details. It makes a safe and accessible way for you to spend and buy bitcoin, Ethereum, and other coins. They can be saved physically on a hard drive such as a USB stick or online in mobile apps that give these services. One such app is the Coinbase wallet. This makes using cryptocurrencies as easy as credit cards.

Online wallets have security risks, so developers are always looking for ways to improve the safety of wallets. In addition, there are always people looking to add other people's cryptocurrencies into their wallets.

To counter this issue, two-factor verification is currently being used. However, the system is not perfect as anyone that has access to your emails and your phone will gain access to the wallet. Also, if hackers can somehow find out your personal information, they can access the wallet as well. These safety risks still reside, but the 'Two-Factor Authentication' has greatly reduced the chances of stealing in the cryptocurrency world.

Two-Factor Authentication or 2FA

This is a security protocol that is now being used to authenticate users to stop hackers from gaining access to bank accounts, websites, and cryptocurrency wallets. The system requires you to provide two ways to identify yourself, making the barrier of entry more fortified.

The 2FA or "Two-Factor Authentication" system is used to make secure online accounts, smartphones, and even smart appliances; stronger. This happens when a customer provides two types of details. Usually, one is their Pin or Personal Identification Number or a password, and the second is their smartphone number or fingerprint. Both are needed to be used together for secure access.

Hopefully, you have a greater understanding of the inner workings of cryptocurrencies and Blockchain, so much so that you are confident enough to invest in them. It is important to know a concept, in and out, before you put your money on them. Cryptocurrencies are extremely simple to understand, and after learning about them, you now know more than some journalists and online crypto-enthusiasts. You can explain to them, in simple terms, how cryptocurrency became popular, what will be its effects on society, and the advantages it will provide in day-to-day life.

The cryptocurrency demand, development, and popularity are on the rise, and it will continue rising, but there are thousands of cryptocurrencies to choose from. Each currency has its unique workings, and sometimes they rise together in the market, and more often, each currency grows and fluctuates independently. Therefore, you need to know before you invest what cryptocurrency works best for you.

Chapter 4: Which One Is Right for Me?

Before you buy your first cryptocurrencies, first establish a goal that you want to achieve with your cryptocurrencies. Once you do this, then you can choose the currency which will best suit your goals. For example, suppose you want to purchase an item from your cryptocurrencies, such as a phone. In that case, bitcoin is the best option because it is the most widely used and accepted cryptocurrency. If you do not want to buy, but play online games without constantly putting your credit card details in, then Ethereum is the cryptocurrency for you.

Research Tools for Cryptocurrency

Cryptocurrencies are unstable forms of investment, and in this industry, every piece of information helps. By using good research tools, you can prepare yourself to make informed decisions. Here are some research websites which will aid in your cryptocurrency's investment venture.

Messari

This is a cryptocurrency data aggregator. You can find colorful and eye-catching graphs and charts. They will give you useful information about trading. The Messari screener sorts all kinds of cryptocurrencies information with customization. All the coin metrics can be seen on one page. It could be prices, market cap, trading volume according to the sector, etc.

You can find out different services when exploring Messari's customizable filters. To analyze different currencies in a particular category. The greatest advantage of using Messari's website is that it is completely free. There is a Messari pro upgrade for only $25 per month, which will unlock all the features of the site.

Glassnode

This is one of the most sophisticated sites for data and metric insights of coins. Glassnode can allow you to use unchain market indicators to search a particular coin. The data provided can help you judge the exchange inflow and outflow. The cryptocurrency world is moving every moment, and you can view what is happening in real-time. You can search the crypto markets by using active addresses. It is also free to use the platform, and there is a pro version of the site.

LunarCrush

This is a social media site for cryptocurrencies and the cryptocurrency community. It is one of the most reliable places to get information. The success of crypto depends upon the perception of the public. Trends have huge effects on coin costs. It would be ideal if you look into all the trends and media regarding crypto, but that is an outstanding task. It is impossible to keep up with all the information; this is where LunarCrush comes in.

The site has a functioning AI (artificial intelligence) and learning machine to smartly categorize information obtained from different pages in social media. The platform uses the gathered data from big social media sites such as Reddit, News, Google searches, popular links, and many more areas.

The statistical decisions given by analyzing a huge information pot such as this one will help you make confident and researched-backed decisions. LunarCrush can be used freely, but if you want to try all the services it can provide, you have to subscribe to a premium version.

Coin Metrics

As the name suggests, the site gives you details about cryptocurrency's metric data. Financial information, market data, index data, and other tools are present to navigate what is happening in the financial aspect of cryptocurrencies. They can help you with quick responses. You can search over 100 assets and over 300 metrics. All the data is presented in charts and graphs, which makes it easier to understand. Once you have found what you are looking for, e.g., a price value chart of Litecoin, then you can download it for future use.

Santiment

This is a research tool that works similarly to Glassnode. The platform provides chain and social media information of more than 1500 coins. You can analyze this data thoroughly to understand the next big price explosion.

CoinGecko

Coinmarketcap is probably the main website you go to look for prices and data aggregation, but CoinGecko is not too far behind. It is one of the largest sites which tracks prices of coins by market caps. There is real-time price viewing of almost 8000 currencies and almost 500 exchanges. Not only coins but tokens are also being tracked and measured. The site gives a detailed report of the cryptocurrency market situation. The platform also provides statistical data from cryptocurrency community polls and surveys from social media giants like Facebook, Twitter, etc. Other hidden gem features can be useful to you. You can get a complete picture of a coin or token by seeing the market fluctuations and public opinions.

CoinMarketCal

The price movements in cryptocurrencies are fast and unpredictable for the most part. There are tons of events and activities going around different currencies. To look out for all the events and news of coins is a difficult task, perhaps even impossible. Coinmarketcal is a platform that informs you about all the events occurring in the cryptocurrency industry. You can view the data on a calendar to know the date and time of events as well. The data has a researched and community-managed system. People can add events, and that event information is later checked. If a person has posted a rack event, the event is then downvoted and eventually disappears, while the true event gets upvotes.

Suppose you are looking at a particular coin and want to know more about what effects a particular event had on the price of the coin. In that case, you can simply search the coin and see the data. By clicking on a time duration, it will tell you all the events scheduled during that period.

Researching tools are important for any investment, whether you are going into stocks, bonds, or EFTs. Before putting your money in a cryptocurrency project, you need to understand the data around the coins you are investing in. Begin your portfolio research by familiarizing yourself with one or two sites mentioned above. These sites give you a detailed picture of the price and market environment. You can easily judge what coin will do better and what coin is going to disappear.

Cryptocurrencies are a great investment, prone to price explosions, but they are also extremely volatile. Because of their extreme price surges, many people get emotional and want to buy some coins themselves. It is understandable to be emotional, but do not put all your savings in cryptocurrencies.

The system of cryptocurrency is not very complicated, but their presence is going to make money transferring, saving, and spending a lot more secure. This revolutionary idea can change the way we look at money. Albeit, you are ready to start investing, but you need to know where and what currency you should invest in before that.

Top Blockchain Companies to Lookout For

Tons of publicly traded companies have adopted blockchain technology and use it to refine their online business systems. They offer blockchain features and services to their consumers and indirectly support the blockchain and cryptocurrency industry. Some companies main focus is on blockchain technology and cryptocurrencies development; some produce Blockchain supported items and services or use them in a way that complements their currently run business

If you want to invest in the cryptocurrency world and get a slice of profit off of blockchain advancement, then here are some amazing stocks to keep in your mind. The names listed below are the top companies as of writing and could change with time. These are:

- NVIDIA
- CME
- Square
- Amazon
- Mastercard
- IBM
- Docusign

Fact

These companies are well-established and thriving businesses. They are especially looking into crypto based technologies that can significantly grow their business with the rise in the popularity of cryptocurrencies.

NVIDIA

This company is one of the most well-known in graphic processing units manufacturing or GPU, in the industry. They are a vital part of different, complex, and simple computerized devices and are used in other areas of technology such as artificial intelligence, self-driving cars or any self-driving vehicles, gaming, entertainment, etc. Graphic processing units (GPUs) are needed to run cryptocurrencies because they are the main hardware that helps in cryptocurrency mining. Miners of crypto coins have GPUs that check the transaction data of the "block." For this task, they are rewarded with new coins that are freshly minted. Because cryptocurrencies are reaching high costs, people's interest in mining has peaked. The company NVIDIA has sold thousands of expensive specialized GPUs to Ethereum miners. Their company will continue to grow with cryptocurrency.

CME

This is a company that is currently leading the globe for exchanges, stocks, securities, etc. This is the only exchange where bitcoin futures contracts are made. Bitcoin and cryptocurrencies are getting more attention, and with it, the prices of bitcoin have reached an outstanding value. CME or CME group uses it to their advantage by charging a small fee for every bitcoin-related transaction on their platform. With advancements in cryptocurrencies, other coins could start being offered at their exchanges as well.

Square

Fintech, which is a successful financial technology company, has a sub-company called Square. This company runs its business by using two of its most important processing systems. One is its payment processing platform that helps small businesses, and the second is its app. The Cash App is a personal payment service provider. In addition, the business has many adjacent operations ranging from money lending to stock trading and e-commerce assistance.

Blockchain is used by Square in two ways. You can buy and sell cryptocurrencies like bitcoin on the Cash App. In 2020, 1.6 billion bitcoins were purchased from this app. The company has its division called Square Crypto, in which projects related to cryptocurrencies are launched regularly.

Amazon

The world's most renowned e-commerce site that almost every American uses is Amazon. This company also has its hands on building the leading cloud infrastructure service called Amazon Web Services or AWS. The system uses Amazon blockchain, which helps consumers make and create their blockchain networks. Many people are expecting Amazon to add Blockchain to its e-commerce payment technology.

Mastercard

Mastercard is a huge deal in payment processing. It has become an outstanding company after years of operations, and its target is to create a cash-free economy. Currently, they focus on issuing and managing debit and credit cards and their transactions. In addition, Mastercard has admitted to a partnership with blockchain company R3 to help them in international money transfers. They have also launched a Crypto Card partner program that allows users to spend cryptocurrencies in markets.

IBM

IBM's growth acceleration is not as profound as it used to be, but it has big events lined up to jump-start its growth again. In the world of Blockchain, the company's Blockchain has helped me develop in their industry and give solutions to their clients. With more and more blockchain-based solutions, their advancement will rise, making cryptocurrencies more popular as well. IBM is trying to create more effective supply chains, which were needed during the Covid Pandemic.

DocuSign

E-signatures are being used more frequently, and DocuSign is one of the leading companies in this area. Its technology and popularity have reached an all-time high during the past few years. E-signatures save time and money and reduce stress on workers. It is estimated that there is a $36 reduction on every transaction when doing business. Now, Docusign has started to take blockchain technology and use it to record contracts. Its CEO has commented many times about the importance of blockchain advancement for the growth of the company.

Choose Your Cryptocurrency

With thousands of coins to buy, you want to make sure that the currency you invest in gives you a good return in the end. Even as you read, more cryptocurrencies are being made and available to the public. Hundreds of cryptocurrencies are indeed being made, but this also highlights that many of them are disappearing and going out of business. Just one decade ago, the entire industry of cryptocurrencies was born, and since then, coins have come and gone, most of them without any notice.

In all these years, Bitcoin has remained the most popular and dominant cryptocurrency till now. The largest and most distributed coin in the world is bitcoins. It is the cryptocurrency that started the trend of digital coins, and it's attracting more and more attention. With attention, bitcoin is also receiving billions of investment dollars, acceptance as payment, and recognition of being a viable security asset. The second-largest cryptocurrency of Ethereum is still very far from bitcoin's fame and success. There are others like Ethereum, which include Zcash, Ripple, etc.

Being the most important of all the cryptocurrencies, Bitcoin looks like the most reliable option out there. When people speak of bitcoin, they simultaneously mean cryptocurrencies as well. Both of them have become culturally synonymous with each other. The press and media have been focusing on bitcoin prices with an eagle's eye, and other currencies are performing better because of it.

The success of other cryptocurrencies, for the most part, is dependent on the popularity of bitcoin. Because of its unique position, your cryptocurrency investment should mainly focus here. Have portions of your investment in other cryptocurrencies as well, but not as big as bitcoins.

To assume that Bitcoin will perform better than others is not just a guess. Most coins that have tried to break into the market have died and forgotten. If you invest in a small cryptocurrency coin, most likely, your wealth will go to zero.

Cryptocurrencies are extremely unstable and susceptible to price volatility. As a result, an investment in a small coin can make you lose all your money. This is the main reason why investors are looking for the next big thing in the blockchain market, such as NFTs.

Fact

NFT are called 'Non-Fungible Tokens.' They are one-of-a-kind coins that store some data that cannot be changed and are saved in an online ledger. The data can store pictures, photos, audio, etc.

Chapter 5: The Danger Zone of Investing in Cryptocurrency

The future of cryptocurrencies is bright and has the potential to make extreme profits, but you have to be careful in this industry. Bitcoin and most other cryptocurrencies are decentralized digital currencies that use extreme cryptography and blockchain to ensure transactions are secure and their data safely stored. Blockchain acts as a ledger, a computerized transaction information book. The transactions are recorded in the blockchain. The recorded data is constantly reviewed by cryptocurrency users, which makes it difficult to hack and change stored information. Still, there are other ways hackers attack cryptocurrencies. Hackers and other cybercriminals steal cryptocurrencies by accessing the digital wallets of users.

Fact

A hacker is a person or a group of people that find weaknesses in a system and create security risks like allowing unauthorized access. The weakness can be in hardware or software, but once inside the system, they can do whatever they want.

Peer to Peer (P2P)

Peer-to-peer transactions are currently on the rise due to bitcoins popularity and the introduction of other cryptocurrencies. A peer-to-peer economy is in which people exchange, buy and sell, products or services with each other privately. One person sells the item, and then, the item is directly purchased by the second person who intends to use it for themselves, with no one in between them. Between the two people, there is no third-party entity. In a peer-to-peer transaction, the buyer will transfer the money of the product or service directly to the seller as delivery of payment. The seller in these cases is a private individual or an independent contractor. The seller has ownership of both the means of production and their product. For example, buying food at a local restaurant. They make the product, and you pay them directly for that product.

We hope that businesses act in "good conduct." Cryptocurrencies can code good conduct into the technology, making it unchangeable and transparent. The technology is coded to record only the transaction information and not any other private detail. It does not allow the information to be changed, not even by itself. The system makes sure no one other than the coin's original wallet holders have access to the coins. An application, technology, or machine is not greedy and safe from moral hazard.

Cryptocurrency is Safe, Right??

It's the start of a new decade, and we have seen cryptocurrencies exploding all the time. It looks like anyone who has invested in them is turning rich, and you are watching from the sidelines. It is a great idea to rebalance your portfolio and add bitcoin and other cryptocurrencies to it as well, but if you want to bet everything on them, then you need to be knowledgeable about its risks first.

Cryptocurrencies are reaching outstandingly high figures that nobody could have predicted 10 years ago. This does not mean that you put all your life savings here. Many investors show profits, but everyone has a similar chance of loss. Here are the reasons why investing in cryptocurrency is not a perfect plan.

Volatile

All types of cryptocurrencies are extremely volatile. This is due to the fact that they are relatively new forms of currency and also new in the market space. In this young form, the prices can see peaks and troughs, sometimes in minutes. It makes dealing with it a very risky decision. When a currency's fundamentals are established, there would be no problem, but bitcoins fundamentals are not well defined as of yet.

When you decide on an investment venture, you look at previous years' performance, showing its highs and lows. For example, Bitcoin reached a mark of almost 20 thousand dollars at the end of 2017. Nowadays, it is marked up to 50 thousand dollars. This may sound too good to you, but you need to look at all the history to make a good decision. In just three more months, in 2018, the price of bitcoin dropped below the 7-thousand-dollar markup. Imagine if it had stayed down for longer, then the investors would have fallen into ruin. By looking at its history, there is a good chance that it will drop again.

Cryptocurrency Is not a Replacement For Money

People believe crypto is like money; the more you have it, the more things you can buy with it, etc. It is true that it is working to make a replacement for money, but not right now. Gold and silver coins back in the day were safe to trade because they were backed up by how useful these precious metals were. Local currencies have their governments backing their value. Cryptocurrency is risky because it is not backed up by anything or any group. It is only valuable because people believe it is and use it with each other. The more people accept it and use it with each other, the more value it gets. On days when the transactions with crypto are decreased, the value also decreases. It is completely decentralized with no regulatory body or government helping it. The value is determined by the people that use it, and you can technically say that it has a "made up" value. It is not a stretch to think crypto might disappear after a year or so. Suppose one day people decide not to trust them anymore and stop using them altogether. In that case, its value will turn to zero, and no one will see that coin again.

Not As Safe As You Think

Most people interested in cryptocurrencies say that it is a currency that can take the place of fiat currency after the financial system fails society. Those coins such as Ethereum, will come to the rescue after national banks collapse. However, after the global pandemic of 2020, it has become clearer that they will not be a haven in these situations. All claims of it being a great savior are probably false.

In the occurrence of fiat currencies or the current financial system going down, then governments and banks will start using the old method of holding precious metals as assets to back up the currency and not focus on any cryptocurrency.

A fiat currency collapse is unlikely, but even if a collapse of such a scale happens, it is presumptuous to assume that electricity, the internet, and the power grid would stay the same. There will be no way for anyone to use crypto ever again. In the case of natural disasters, the first thing to get cut off is electricity, so it is unlikely that they can help in this situation.

Other Risks of Cryptocurrencies

Blockchain technology has made transactions inherently more safe, but that does not mitigate the risks of dealing with money online. Digital money is not tangible; it is transferred and accounted for by computer systems and processes that run it. Any problems here can result in the loss of your hard-earned coins. They have multiple risks attached to them. Here are the 10 main risks of cryptocurrencies.

Low Barrier of Entry

Among the 1500 cryptocurrencies that have been circulating because of the internet, only a handful of cryptocurrencies, such as Ethereum and Litecoin, have gained enough popularity to make people's heads turn. These currencies have been digitally minted and made up by the general public, essentially democratizing this finance feature. Lots of people enter the scene by their digital coin, with prices experiencing highs and lows. Most of the time, they do not recover from the difficult times, but it is very difficult to exit the industry. In sales, hundreds of people rush in the shops, only to get trampled and hurt when they try to rush out of the store. It is the same with cryptocurrencies. The exit is narrowed because of limited technology, inconvenience, and fewer people to trade with.

Intangible

Cryptocurrencies are not only intangible, but it is hard to turn them into stable money, and they are not insured. The innovativeness of blockchain technology and cryptocurrencies is that they remove the issue of double counting. This is resolved without the oversight of third parties like banks and their employees. The reason why it became so popular is that it proposed the notion of digital singularity. It gave the idea to people that society, because of cryptocurrencies, can see out of control and irreversible technological growth in the future that we cannot even comprehend at this time. The popularity of cryptocurrencies showed that an asset can be determined by one instance. This idea made an asset or, in this case, cryptocurrencies powerful.

Its advantages aside, the nature of crypto is illiquid and intangible. Both of these negative features block its ability to be insured and converted easily. Nevertheless, there is extreme interest by the people, and hundreds of companies are emerging. Still, most of them are not insured or cannot be insured. For established industries, there is a deposit insurance "floor" that ensures investor security. However, because cryptocurrencies lack this floor or base limit for being insured, crypto companies and token companies cannot get a wide appeal from investors.

Fact

Double counting is an error seen in economics because of faulty calculation. It can be a result of incorrect counting of a nation's goods.

Not Working with The Market

For cryptocurrencies to stop being intangible, it is to enter the asset in the fiat currencies category. This idea is not well-liked by cryptocurrency users and purists. Making the asset more safe or more liquid means relying on U.S. dollars or banks. When buying coins, it is easy to accept the fact that cryptocurrencies can rise and fall whenever and understand that, as investors, they are taking risks. But when selling, dealing with current market value and lower prices make investors not only realize how big these problems are but make them susceptible to downward price pressure. These adverse effects can be decreased by getting more investors, institutions, markets, and trading platforms open to cryptocurrencies. Until the above happens, you have to keep in mind that the currency is hard to convert, subject to volatility.

Fact

Volatility in science is the ability of a solid substance to directly turn into gas. In economics, it means extreme changes in price and value.

Misinformation

The first rule that all investors should follow, whether new or old, is that they should never invest any money they are unprepared to part ways with. A second rule everyone should follow is that you should know fully the investment process and all the features it provides you, no matter how small the amount may be. Unfortunately, cryptocurrencies are especially susceptible to naive populations who do not fully understand these rules. Malicious people can take advantage of the analog economy and trick confused and unknowledgeable individuals into extortion, market manipulation, fraud, etc. SEC (U.S. Securities and

Exchange Commission) have created their own fake coin to make people aware of cyber crimes around cryptocurrencies. Attention to security details and debate about the safety of completely decentralized coins such as Ethereum, which cannot be controlled with company-run coins, are still a hot topic.

Fact

Cryptocurrency can be stolen. In the early 2010s, the value of bitcoin was growing with acceleration, which garnered a lot of attention from hackers. The website Mt. Gox was attacked, and bitcoin worth about $30,000 was stolen. The website recovered from this setback and became the largest handler of cryptocurrencies, handling 70% of all bitcoin transfers.

In 2014, a major hack was attempted at the Mt.Gox website in which the stolen bitcoin worth was $460,000,000. This was the biggest theft in bitcoin history. This massive hack caused the value of bitcoin to plummet by half, and it took two more years till it went back to its old place again

Protection From Hacks

Cryptocurrencies have a lot of problems, such as intangibility and illiquidity, but the biggest risk of all is custody and control of already obtained coins. Banks have high-level physical and cyber security, but there are essentially mini wars taking place in the cryptocurrency world. Hackers are constantly attacking digital wallets, and custodians are trying out new security settings to counteract them. High-end cryptocurrency users are doing their best to provide the highest standard of protection. Still, a set-in-stone security protocol has yet to be established. The wealthy can place their physical and digital wallets in offline or airtight vaults, but not every average user can use such methods even though all consumers of coins are targets. There is a base or floor of security standards that give guarantees and a type of insurance to consumers. Unfortunately, the cryptocurrency industry lacks such a floor. FDIC (Federal Deposit Insurance Corporate) cannot protect crypto investors.

Risks Of Being on The Internet

When you deal with money online, there are cyber-attacks from every corner. According to Moore's law, computers' capacity to calculate and compute is increasing exponentially, and so is the ability to hack our digital wallets. With it, we have to keep modifying our security systems as well. Blockchains' biggest advantage is that the data stored within does not change easily. Therefore, it is one of the most cyber-resilient inventions. However, many cyber security companies fail to check and monitor the growth of hacker technology and also not upgrade their vaults.

Each cryptocurrency is made differently, with separate levels of traceability and ledgering. They also have different levels of trust and fiduciary responsibility. Because of them, simple risks of disappearances of coins can occur, and complex risks such as cyber ransomware threats are a big possibility. Intelligent software and scour for weakly guarded wallets and attack them as they are easy targets.

Little Mistakes Can Cost a Fortune

A digital wallet is only accessible via a password, so something as common as password amnesia can make you lose all your cryptocurrency coins. Some people have been lucky. People who had gotten bitcoin as a joke or as an out-of-the-box gift, only to find out that the money has turned into a fortune a decade later. But there are risks of forgetting, such as being locked out, facing faulty hardware, and simple action of spilling your coffee, that can cause greater losses. There is always a buyer's risk because of the volatility of cryptocurrencies. It can make them emotional and make bad decisions. Because blockchain technology is open to the public eye, any high-profile transactions can attract physical harm to a person, such as kidnapping, ransom, and extortion. If you become successful, then buying a Lamborghini will not help either.

Fact

Password amnesia is extremely common. You see people forgetting passwords every day. In fact, a study found that almost 80% of users forget their passwords and go for a reset. That means 8 out of every 10 people.

Not A Haven

Being a relatively new industry, and its laws and regulatory limits are not yet set in stone. Changes are occurring every month and most of them without the general public's attention. As a result, there is miscommunication, unclear laws, and complex tax and legal treatment.

The slow movement of regulatory bodies has made the quality of law poor. The government and politics did not even look at cryptocurrencies until the rise of bitcoin in 2017. After that explosion, the globe has become a cryptocurrency hub, where everyone is trying to get a piece of profit as soon as possible. It is a globally run financial system; coordination between countries outside boundaries is important but also cripplingly slow. If these mundane practices are solved, then cryptocurrencies can get near stability.

Limitations of Technology

As previously discussed, it takes a lot of energy to mine bitcoin, and reports have started to pile up, proving its energy consumption problem. There is also the computation complexity around cryptocurrencies. These are just some examples of limitations of technology with crypto.

The complexity provides safety but has some negative consequences as well. They render a threat to this asset class because complex computation means that the problems arising are also extremely complicated. A true blockchain can be defined as decentralized and free of disasters and a risk-free environment, but all cryptocurrencies are true blockchains. They all might mitigate the risks of a breach, which causes massive data losses, but not every token or coin is perfect. For this reason, you as an investor should be aware of technology risks and should research whether a coin or token gives you all the benefits of blockchain.

Forks and Disputes

Cryptocurrency enthusiasts are the main consumers of cryptocurrencies, and much of crypto wealth is in their hands. They believe in the future where this asset class is going in a bright direction and constantly have positive feedback about its acceptance into society. They are optimistic, but it does not look good when mini civil wars occur within a coin. Major disagreements in cryptocurrency communities regarding laws and changes in features can cause "forks" or bifurcation. This cuts the market value of the currency significantly and discourages people from venturing into the industry. The most popular fork in history is when bitcoin was divided into bitcoin and bitcoin cash. A more recent fork would be Ethereum's "London" hard fork in August 2021. Cryptocurrencies enthusiasts can talk about a utopia where money is safe and does not need to be guarded, but they are the main drivers of price fluctuations and outcomes. Just as whales eat up small fishes, these enthusiasts can eat up small investors by manipulating the markets.

With great rewards comes great risks as well. It is because of these risks that the price explosions occur, and people gain profits. Unlike acting as a risk-taking teenager, you can look into the details and make good long-term decisions about your portfolio and adoption of cryptocurrencies.

Crypto as a Property

Cryptocurrencies, as discussed before, are not an alternative to money. The local currency rules do not apply to bitcoin, Ethereum, or any other coin or token. They are classified as property rather than proper currencies by the IRS in the United States. This is how the central authoritative bodies view cryptocurrencies.

This means that the property of cryptocurrency is subject to capital tax, and you have to report your cryptocurrencies expenses and profits yearly, whether you bought new coins or not.

The U.S. taxpayer is already extremely confused, and adding a layer of more complex laws to cryptocurrencies has made them even harder. Some aspects of the laws are not even clear as of right now. For example, it is not defined whether an investor needs to report their coin holdings in foreign exchanges or not. However, a report by a news channel showed that if you have more than $10,000 worth of coins abroad, then you need to report it by filling out a form of FBAR (Foreign Banks and Financial Accounts) annually. In another place, it is said that the FATCA (Foreign Account Tax Compliance Act) requires all U.S cryptocurrency investors to show their overseas accounts when they file for taxes with the IRS.

License and Registration

Cryptocurrencies businesses have been growing in number, and they are taking advantage of the popularity of cryptocurrencies. However, as in every other industry, businesses in this class of industry need to be registered and get a license to perform operations and provide services.

Unfortunately, because of the complexity revolving around digital currencies and changing laws and legal status, it is not a defined process, and limitations are not set for business operations.

Businesses that will only deal with cryptocurrencies may not need to get a license or even register themselves. However, they are required to file a special consideration depending on which state they belong to. The business has the entire control for managing and maintaining security status and regulations of legal procedures at both national and state levels. An example would be that a federal business must follow the rules and work against money laundering and fraud. It is their job to monitor and report such transactions taking place. This rule also applies to financial institutions such as digital currencies.

Illegal Activities with Cryptocurrencies

There are big believers in the mainstream community that cryptocurrencies help criminals and criminal organizations by helping them commit fraud, money laundering, and other financial crimes. However, a big portion of the population is turned off by this idea and does not intend to use a new complex technology that criminals use. In addition to this, investors may not have the same standings as someone who uses fiat currency when falling victim to a financial crime. This is because laws are still unfinished and lagging.

Fact

Computer lagging is used to describe a situation when an application is running slow on a computer.

When an account is hacked in a traditional bank, the crime is reported, investigated, and the money is traced. You can, at the end of the day, get your money back. However, because of the decentralized nature of cryptocurrencies, an investor takes on a risk that their money cannot be recovered in case of theft of their coin holdings and exchange. Missing funds cannot be traced with an asset class of cryptocurrencies.

For these reasons, cryptocurrencies investors and developers are looking for ways to create a better and effective system to hold digital coins. New wallets and innovations around its security are constantly upgraded and updated, but they are still not able to completely block the legal risks of losing data, and they may never. On a positive note, governments, financial institutions, and national and central banks are trying to understand digital currencies' workings, appeal, and features.

At the end of the day, there are risks in all forms of investment; it is up to you whether you are willing to take both losses and gains of the asset. As a future investor, you should be relieved to find out that the markets and those who focus on exchanges are regulated. If a problem arises and you have a dispute that needs to be settled, then you will be supplied with a regulatory audience. With cryptocurrencies, this is not the case. You may be on your own on this investment. It all depends upon your tolerance to risk. If you understand all the risks and still want to continue, then there is no shame in doing so. Hundreds of people took risks years ago that are now living happy lives. That person can be you too.

Keeping Your Coins Secure

This is an important step after you buy your coins and save them into your wallet. It is even more important when choosing to use your coins to actively buy items on the internet or save them in a hot wallet. Every time you purchase an item with cryptocurrency coins, then you need to be certain that your investment is safe. For this, it is advised that you use a VPN.

Many VPN companies, such as NordVPN or ExpressVPN, help you stay anonymous and keep your data encrypted. When you use a Virtual Private Network, your online connections become secure, and one can see your data, not even your internet provider. Having your data encrypted can mean that online transactions and the information attached to them can be safely hidden. Think of it as an extra layer of protection for the coins and the purchases you will make online. In addition, this network will make it more difficult for thieves and hackers to log on to your device. There is many more VPN software out there that you can choose to make your devices more secure.

Risks and Volatility

Every cryptocurrency acts differently, and if one coin rises in price, it does not mean the other will as well. Each coin has unique features that dictate the price swing. If you are investing in a coin, it is very important to know as much about that coin as possible before investing. You should know why the coin or token was created, what problem it is trying to solve, what governance structure it runs on, and its performance last year. The more you understand it, the more you will approach it better. For example, suppose you are thinking about investing in the top two performing cryptocurrencies. In that case, you should know that bitcoin acts like gold because it has a finite supply of coins and can be used to beat inflation. This cannot be done by Ethereum. So, you choose Bitcoin over Ethereum using this logic.

Digital coins are labeled as alternative assets and have not been given a category of their own yet. Like real estate or commodities, they are a way to diversify your portfolio, and diversity is good in investment. They have a low correlation with other assets, meaning, if one asset goes down, it is unlikely that cryptocurrencies will, too, because they work in different sectors.

Cryptocurrencies are volatile because their trade is active 24/7 and all days of the year. This makes people react quickly according to the news and even tweets. Therefore, you need to be able to embrace volatility if you want substantial gains.

Once you have invested and saved up your coins in a secure wallet, then you will need to check on them from time to time and even add some changes to your portfolio. This will be discussed more in the next chapter.

Chapter 6: How Do I Get in On the Action?

There are two different ways you can profit off cryptocurrency. One is to directly buy some well-performing crypto coins and save them in your wallet. The price of these coins will rise with the rise of their popularity and usage. The second way is to invest in companies related to cryptocurrencies and use their technology in some shape or form. To be able to identify well-performing coins and companies, you have to first do thorough research on every option that is available. By using the websites mentioned in Chapter 5, you can identify the market trend, whether it is rising or declining. You will decide which cryptocurrencies and companies, use cryptocurrency technology to invest in with this information and when. Investing is a game of chance only when you blindly place your bets. By putting a little time and effort before choosing and investing your money, you will decrease the chances of losing any capital. Using different websites and resources makes well-informed and calculated decisions that can lead you to a good life.

You cannot skip researching, especially when you are a first-time investor and have just entered the crypto world. Using apps and websites like Messari, Glassnode and

Lunarcrush can place you above hundreds of other people. Placing your money in an unsafe, volatile environment can be stressful and difficult, so you have to be very confident in the choices you have made. Choose a high-level coin such as Ethereum or Dogecoin. Always be ready for any setbacks and never invest money you are not ready to lose. Following this advice will help you be stress-free and be less emotional. In addition, they will make taking every step feel easy and not daunting. The first step is always difficult, but you will always be filled with regret if you do not take action.

Where To Buy Cryptocurrencies?

Through online connections, it is extremely easy to acquire any kind of cryptocurrency. The most common and least complex way to get your hands on some coins is through online exchanges, for example:

- Coinbase
- Binance
- Kraken
- Bitstamp, etc.

On these online exchange websites, you can buy whatever major crypto coin you like. Minor and less popular cryptocurrencies are difficult to get because fewer people are interested in them and are unstable. The major currencies available of these online exchanges are:

- Bitcoin or BTC
- Litecoin or LTC
- Ethereum or ETH
- Bitcoin Cash or BCH
- Ethereum Classic or ETC

Some exchanges can give you the chance to buy emerging cryptocurrencies like Stellar Lumens or EOS.

Some of these online exchanges allow you to get some coins for free such as Coinbase. You can get some of these free coins and explore the different services provided by the exchanges. This will let you know the full procedure of buying and saving before actually putting in dollars, making you more comfortable.

One great feature about online exchanges is that some of them allow you to buy portions of a coin. That means you do not need to buy the entire coin. If you are short on money but still want to invest in some cryptocurrencies, then you can buy portions of them for as little as 5 dollars. The websites not only take dollars but euros, pounds, and other local currencies as well.

You do not need to buy cryptocurrencies by directly buying them. Instead, you can invest in some companies that run crypto for a good profit.

Cryptocurrencies technology is based on the Blockchain – a decentralized system that makes it impossible to counterfeit and change the data. Companies are trying to educate their staff and the customers because this form of payment is increasing in popularity fast. It can be an important step for companies to start introducing new policies related to the advantages of Blockchain. There are features and benefits that they provide, which fiat currencies cannot.

Platforms That Sell Cryptocurrencies

As said before, cryptocurrencies cannot be bought via banks or traditional brokers but by their dedicated websites. They are called Crypto Investing Exchange and function as online cryptocurrency brokers. They will act as a crypto coin seller to you. It is a bit of a setback that you cannot purchase them at your regular investment and financial places, and when buying cryptocurrencies, you will be only limited to their services, but these exchanges will serve your crypto needs well.

There are hundreds of bid platforms out there, but the best ones are described below:

Coinbase

This company started its operations in 2012 when cryptocurrencies were still a radical idea. They allowed people to transfer and receive Bitcoins. Now, the company is one of the first picks of crypto enthusiasts to buy some cryptocurrencies. It has an easy-to-navigate interface and a wide range of coins to choose from.

Gemini

Selling cryptocurrencies is something all cryptocurrency exchanges can provide, but Gemini is a unique website that allows you to save your coins in a digital wallet as well. Researching and other different tools that you might need to buy the best cryptocurrencies are available. You will also earn risk-free, 7.4% interest just for using Gemini's wallet to store your coins.

Unifimoney

This website offers you more diverse services that you would not normally see in other exchanges. It provides banking, investing, and financial assistance as well. You can also store some cryptocurrencies from other partner exchanges in a unifimoney account. If you want all of your financial workings to be in one place, then this is the site.

Binance

Binance is a globally run company with many branches, including Binance.US. They have one of the lowest charges on trading and other types of exchanges. Unfortunately, it does not allow you to add other cryptocurrencies from different exchanges. However, they are still on the top in cryptocurrency exchanges.

Robinhood

All of the financial institutions refuse to deal with cryptocurrencies, except for one. That one gives you the chance to buy coins alongside your investment brokers. That company is called Robinhood. It is a certified investment broker provider. Most of the time, these types of businesses run on commissions, but not Robinhood. You can shop for stocks, ETFs, and cryptocurrencies that will all be commission-free.

Fact

The full form of the ETF is an Exchange Traded Fund. These funds are a type of stock that follows the market and diversifies your portfolios quickly. You can learn more about them in my previous book "Making More Money for YOU!

Mutual Fund Investing on a Budget for Beginners".

Robinhood has a wide array of coins for you to choose from, including bitcoin, bitcoin cash, Ethereum, Litecoin, etc. They are less pricey and easy to keep your eye on. Here, cryptocurrencies are not the only way you can invest in cryptocurrencies and blockchain technology. A reminder that the website does not use crypto to run its business; it simply gives a platform to people trying to learn about them.

There are many other cryptocurrency exchanges on the internet where you can get your cryptocurrencies from.

Fact

A moral hazard is an action done by an individual that is harmful or risky in some way without regard to consequences.

Investing in Cryptocurrencies

Bitcoin has seen price explosions, which has led to people looking at cryptocurrencies as an investment. The price explosion occurred in 2017 and then again in 2021. The people who had bought cryptocurrencies before these times can attest that it was the best investment they have ever made. The road is still far ahead, and cryptocurrencies have a long way to go till it becomes recognized as a valuable currency everywhere. Price explosions are expected to occur shortly as well.

Cryptocurrencies investment is not something you can do at your local banks and brokerage firms. Cryptocurrencies have become popular, but mostly with the younger generation. Financial institutions have not yet accepted cryptocurrencies as a typical business. Because of a lack of information and regulations, financial institutions do not offer their services. For this reason, cryptocurrencies run on their own ecosystem. To start investing here is some advice to follow:

- Place a small portion of your portfolio in cryptocurrencies. When you decide to buy cryptocurrencies and stocks related to them, then you will need to choose the percentage it will occupy within your portfolio. Sometimes, it is difficult to come up with a logical decision, especially when you see Bitcoin's prices rise.
- You have to not get emotional here. Emotions such as greed and fear are great hurdles when investing.

Bitcoin's success will make you greedy, but you have to be smart about money.

- Your portfolio should have a small portion of cryptocurrencies. The amount may vary according to the total value of your investment but do not invest more than 5 to 10 percent of it. Cryptocurrencies function separately from stocks, and they have different risks attached to them. It mostly resembles security provided by buying precious metals like silver or gold. However, they do not pay interest or dividends. They are also unstable, and their success only depends upon their ability to rise constantly and remain at the top for a while.

- Cryptocurrency's function does not involve being used as an investment tool. Cryptocurrencies are preferred for easy and safe transferring of money from person to person. And, it has a currency status or is mimicking the currency status, like dollar or pound. Cryptocurrencies are becoming more mainstream because it helps transfer money, a common task, to become much easier, cheaper, and faster. The value of cryptocurrencies is solely governed by the market and not politics like other currencies.

That being said, cryptocurrencies have not yet solidified their standing as a medium of exchange. Of course, thousands of shops accept them, but that is limited if you look at it globally. So, the future is still uncertain, and you should not put all your eggs in one basket.

More On Pipers for Trading

2021 has been a great year for almost all cryptocurrencies. The prices are exploding, and the year is not even over yet. The value of cryptocurrencies has surpassed almost $3 Trillion, and businesses are eager to start using this technology. This year's price rise has encouraged many beginner investors into the crypto industry, fueling further growth and development. A rough estimate indicates that almost 15% of American adults now own some sort of cryptocurrency.

Digital assets, such as cryptocurrencies, are fortunately available on cryptocurrencies exchanges. There are hundreds of them as crypto has gone up in popularity. However, you need to be smart about choosing the right one. Every exchange offers some extra features that you can use to determine which exchange you want to work with. These exchanges are Coinbase, Gemini, etcetera, and in these exchanges, thousands of different coins are available for purchase, whether it be stable or joke coins.

Fact

Dogecoin is the first joke cryptocurrency coin that was introduced in 2013 by two software engineers. It is based on a "doge meme" with Shiba Inu's image on the coin. Despite its satirical nature, its overall value has now reached up to $85 billion, with a dedicated community backing it up. This joke coin is now a legitimate cryptocurrency that many people confidently invest in. Ethereum and tether are two coins that begin as joke coins as well.

Fact

Inflation is the rate at which the prices rise for a particular given period. For example, something that would have cost 5 dollars 10 years ago is worth 12 dollars now. This price increase is credited to inflation. There are many reasons why inflation happens, such as an increase in production cost, an increase in demand, and an increase in wages.

We all want to know a way to safely increase our wealth so that we can have a good retirement. Investment is a great option, probably one of the best options out there. However, cryptocurrencies have not yet been accepted by traditional brokers and even traditional online brokers. It might be popular, but it is not as mainstream as local currencies.

Here is a list of brokers that allow you to have cryptocurrencies in your portfolio, along with stocks and bonds. Their features, services, reviews, and processing fees vary. You can use these factors to choose an online broker for yourself.

Robinhood

This is a commission-free online broker site that is regarded as one of the best online brokers for coin trading. It was on Bankrate's list for best broker for cryptocurrencies trading. The site also comes with an app, which is handy. Its user interface is extremely friendly, meaning it is an easy-to-use application. The broker firm has many great reviews, but it is noteworthy that the site stopped working for a while during the GameStop trading fiasco in 2021.

Sofi Invest

This online broker landed on the best cryptocurrency exchanges list on Nerdwallet. The downside of the site is that it is not commission-free, and it charges a markup of almost 1.25% when doing cryptocurrency transactions. However, they have promotions and schemes going on most of the time, which helps you save up a lot more. For example, the site offered $10 of bitcoin with every $10 trade on cryptocurrencies a while back.

TradeStation

Just like Robinhood, the site was listed as one of the best cryptocurrencies brokers by Bankrate. It is popular among active and advanced traders, meaning you should look at this site after getting some experience in cryptocurrency trading. Again, the downside is that it is not commission-free, starting at 0.3% per trade and dropping in charges once your balance goes higher than $100,000.

Brokers such as TD Ameritrade, Interactive Brokers, and Charles Schwab are traditional brokers that also offer bitcoin futures trading. However, they do not offer other cryptocurrencies.

After you do your homework and look up all the features of the brokers, then you can decide which one to pick. However, if none of them suit you, you should consider using cryptocurrency exchanges. You can start by making an account by signing up and exploring them before you put your money in.

Coinbase

This is the only cryptocurrency online exchange site, and it is the largest one in America. Here you can get over 50 types of coins. It has a commission fee of about 0.5% and another additional fee of almost $0.99 for partaking in transactions and using digital coins and tokens.

Gemini

Here you can buy more than 40 digital coins, slightly less than Coinbase, and the charges for transactions are nearly 1.49%. Of course, this value can change depending on what trading platforms you are using.

eToro

This site is a social trading platform where you can trade with over 20 cryptocurrencies. In addition, there are options to use other assets for people living outside the U.S. The spread varies, but for bitcoin, it starts at 0.75%. eToro is one of the best cryptocurrency investment sites and also one of the most advanced. It offers unique services and features, such as CopyTrader Technology. Using the feature, you can copy the investment strategies and portfolio from the most successful crypto traders on the site at the time. It also has features similar to Roboto advisors. The feature is called CopyPortfolios, which acts as a professional portfolio manager.

Fact

ARobotoadvisor is an artificial intelligence (AI) driven application or software that gives financial advice and is used in investing.

eToro also helps you learn and explore investing in cryptocurrencies by offering virtual portfolios where you can trade over $100,000 on a paper account without using any money. This will help you learn the ropes before you start saving and storing money in cryptocurrency.

Chapter 7: When Do You Check on These Things and What Do I Use to Check on Them?

Investing in cryptocurrency can be seen as a clever short-term investment rather than a long-term investment that is provided by traditional stock exchanges. This is because the cryptocurrency industry is relatively new and extremely impressionable by influencers and tech enthusiasts. Banks and stock exchanges are not yet comfortable enough to add them as an option for trading, and you should also vary the future of cryptocurrencies. Checking can be healthy, but it is about checking properly and managing efficiently.

Why can cryptocurrencies not be treated as long-term investments?

Long-term investments grow at a steady rate, generally. Many people have tried and tested these investments that have come before you and are safer than regular investments. These investments grow without much intervention from the investor. There have been instances where elderly men and women forgot that they had invested a humble amount of money in their youth, only to find out later that the sum of money had turned into something substantial. Cryptocurrency has only been in the market for two decades and what will happen after 40 years is still a mystery.

Fact

Long-term investments are investments that somebody or some company plans to hold for more than three years.

Cryptocurrency as a Short-term Investment

Short-term investments are mainly sorted out by individuals for quick gains, just like what. For them, you will have to check on the market from time to time. The price will be different, one day, it will be high, and the next, it can be struggling. Sometimes the news and industry cryptocurrencies are stable enough that checking on it once or twice a week is all that is needed. However, some days, due to some event or even some tweet, the market becomes unstable again, and you have to refresh your stocks page several times a day to make a quick gain.

A cryptocurrency investor such as you should not only look at the stocks of businesses that use cryptocurrencies, but you need to keep a close eye on the market capitalization of the coin you have bought or invested in. First, you have to check the amount of trade happening with your coin. When people start using a digital coin more often, its value increases. If people show disinterest in your invested coin and fewer trades are happening with that coin, then the overall value of that coin decreases.

Many people on the internet tell others to check their portfolio and coin value every hour and even every minute. You will stumble upon such advice on social media websites such as Facebook, Reddit, YouTube, etc. Unfortunately, hundreds of people check their portfolio and coin value hundreds of times a day, mostly with no actual benefit. Checking any of your investments, including crypto investments, will be detrimental to your mental and physical health. This is an unrealistic strategy that has no proper advantage associated with it.

Keeping Up with Media Is Important

It is not advisable to check your numbers multiple times a day, but it is beneficial to check them once daily. You should look out for any acceleration in the movement of cryptocurrencies. News articles can drive the prices of digital coins. Serious contenders like Bitcoin, Ethereum to joke coins such as Dogecoin, and other small crypto coins and tokens can be affected positively or negatively by trending news. This can be seen by looking at bitcoin. The cryptocurrency has gone to a positive surge in 2016 because of good news and comments said about it by influential people and businesses.

On the other hand, it felt a downward surge as news articles started publishing negative reports. This uncertainty is what makes crypto experience great volatility. So, you have to keep an eye on the news as well.

Treat Cryptocurrency as a Volatile Asset

Even if you are a casual user of cryptocurrencies and use it to buy items online and do online transactions, you need to be informed about the value of the coins you are using and know whether it has increased or decreased. Cryptocurrency enthusiasts, investors, speculators, and other curious people will constantly ask questions about the frequency at which they should check their assets and asset performance.

Fact

Assets are any resource that is owned by or controlled by an individual or organization. They are seen as a representation of value, and their value can be converted to cash by the individual or organization that owns it.

Common examples of assets are cars, houses, investments, artwork, heavy machinery, jewelry, and patents.

Regardless of whether you want to check the performance of a cryptocurrency for curiosity, purchasing, or investing purposes, the market is the best way to make decisions about the coin. To make the best decisions on what to do with your cryptocurrencies, you need to look at the movement of your coin in the market. Identify when the coin is selling at a high rate or when the price is rising so that you can capitalize on them and sell your coins for massive returns.

Cryptocurrency is extremely volatile, so investors and people holding it as a commodity should have impeccable timing. There can be many reasons why a coin is doing unwell one day when it was on the rise before. Digital coins and tokens carry a lot of their worth based on how many users they have, the designs behind them, and the problem they are trying to solve.

The value can be fluctuated by external factors as well, something that they are not in control of. Therefore, any time of the day is a good time to check up on them because their price changes determine their performance, which can happen at any time of the day. Some important occasions when you absolutely must check the performance of your coins are during a financial collapse, trending of any cryptocurrency-related news, and globally affected disasters such as a pandemic. Such events can have a significant impact on them, and you might miss out on an opportunity of a lifetime if you are not looking out for the news.

How Often Should You Check Cryptocurrency Market?

The birth of cryptocurrencies can be accredited to the failure of the global economic system and the stock market crash. This collapse builds more confidence in the public to try out new currencies and start accepting digital coins. This confidence is what makes the prices of cryptocurrencies increase from time to time. The loss of trust in banks and other big financial cooperation directly influences digital coins and tokens. The prices of cryptocurrencies also decreased during the Coronavirus pandemic in 2020, along with other fiat currencies. We can infer from previous experiences that during moments of crisis, you should check the value of cryptocurrencies because they often rapidly deplete at those times.

Looking At the News Is Not Enough

If you are looking at the numbers for a long time, chances are that you have noticed that a period of high-value increase is preceded by a depreciation of the price. This behavior of any commodity, including cryptocurrencies, is long proven by financial experts and analysts. For example, when you hear the news of Bitcoin and know that its value has increased, a few days later, that same coin decreases in value. The value may be insignificant enough that the media does not cover it, but it always happens. Similarly, when the price falls, at one point, they are at the lowest they can go before rising to a certain level as well. This behavior of commodities in the market is called a self-correction mechanism. It is the resistance of momentum or resistance of change. It is, therefore, necessary that you not only look at the news but also observe the factors that can affect the movement of cryptocurrencies.

Other Factors You Have to Check

Critical insights and analysis about the factors that affect the value of your coin are also essential. You will need to be ready to use different tools and applications to give more detail about those factors. The applications and good habits formed with them will not only make you well informed but also ensure that you never miss an opportunity to make a profit. One tool that you can use is an application you can place on your phone called Myfxbook. It will keep you updated and well-informed about different factors that affect your coin's value. In addition, you will be getting analysis reports from professionals whose job is to track cryptocurrencies.

This is a great way to use your resources and critical thinking to get ahead in the market. However, another great tool to use is an investing dot com website. They give a wide array of pinpoint updates about any commodity. Users and investors of cryptocurrencies can create an account or subscribe to get expert insights and their views.

We all live busy lives, with family and jobs to look after. You might not be related to the financial industry at all and have no clue what decisions to make just by looking at numbers or hearing the news. Because of this, you might think having an expert's opinion about the digital coin market can be very helpful.

You do not always need to pay a third party for news. This is just to make things easy. You can yourself become an expert in looking at cryptocurrencies by looking at the numbers, news, expert opinions on the news, and social media. However, it will take time until you become confident in your decisions.

Tools can also help you notice a rise or fall of specific coins and tokens, e.g., Bitcoin, by giving a notification every time it happens. You can set your apps to send you notifications when changes occur, and this way, you will be well informed and not ever need to open the application to check value by yourself.

You can check the value and stock numbers of the cryptocurrency sector every day. Still, if you set up your tools smart enough, you can make this experience as pain-free as possible. Remember not to get overwhelmed, emotional and paranoid. Do not check the numbers so often that it gives anxiety.

There are many schools of thought on the frequency of checking your numbers. This will ultimately depend upon your passion, dedication, and interest. You may use multiple apps to keep you posted. You can also watch a channel with an expert that gives you their opinions on the subject while giving you all the trends of cryptocurrencies happening at that moment. Finally, you can set a time of the day to look at the numbers on investing websites.

In investing, you must look at the investment's performance. You have put your hard-earned money on the line; the least you can do is know how well your coin is doing and how much money is being generated. By being informed, you can make a good strategy and maximize the profit. If you want to make gains, you need to put in a little effort. Fortunately, with the crypto industry giving opportunities after opportunities, it will not be that difficult to make those gains.

Improve Your Checking Habits

This market needs to be checked often, but you can save some of your precious time by employing useful methods. To improve your habits, you need to follow the steps given below.

- Have a strategy

   Temptations will always be present, and the urge to check on your money is very persuasive. However, if you are experiencing FOMO or fear of missing out, then you need to start taking small steps to fix your behavior. According to your schedule, limit the time you will spend monitoring your numbers and dedicate a specific time for it. For example, if you go to work in the morning and commute by bus, the best time to check is when you are coming back home from work.

- Think long term

   In the fast-pacing world of cryptocurrencies, 1 or 2 years can feel like a lifetime. Investing and money-making is a game of patience and seizing opportunity when it strikes. Remember all the strategies and tools you have placed to give you confidence. Do not get emotional and start to panic when the price drops. Remember why you started investing in the first place. Think about your financial goals and be cool and collected when the prices are swinging. Look at the bigger picture; you took this risk for a reason. To help you remain calm, it is important to put only the money you are ready to lose in the first place. Never put your savings on the line for a quick buck.

- Seek assistance

  If you know that the temptation of checking your crypto rates is too much, then ask for someone's help. You can seek professional assistance by consulting a financial advisor or seeing an expert and asking them for advice. You could also have a roommate, or family member hold you accountable or for falling into your bad habits. Choose the one the suits you the best and the one that can remove your behavior better

There are times when you can leave your investing to experts, but this is a practice followed by traditional stock exchanges, and the cryptocurrency sector has yet to solidify its position there.

Important Advice to Always Remember

Cryptocurrencies as an investment class is a new concept, and because very little data is present for fundamental performance analysis, it is termed as a risky proposition. This is a high reward and a high-risk arena. Here are some essential facts to keep in mind when your money moves in the cryptocurrency's hotpot.

- Do not take the whole cake when all you want is a slice

  The returns that crypto gives can be mouth-watering, and you can lose your senses when you see lucky crypto investors in their fancy cars and extravagant houses. In just this past one-year, people have gained enough profits to set them up for life, and this phenomenon is not only seen in bitcoin. The digital joke currency Dogecoin has risen 50 times more than at the beginning of the year. These values are insane but do not be carried away by them. Invest only the money you are willing to lose. Even if you want to trade with higher values and money, start tracing with humble amounts first. Have a category separate from savings called investments in your budget and only allocate 2% of that to cryptocurrencies. After a few months, once you get a good knowledge of the crypto market, how to read numbers, other coins, and tokens, and develop healthy habits, then start to allocate more.

- Do not jump ships when tides are high

  Once you have put some money into crypto coins, you will start gaining experiences and lessons. In a high-risk game, you should have the stomach to take heavy losses and or even be calm when prices surge low. An overnight sudden fall of 80% of a coin's value is very possible. The chances of the waves turning the opposite way are also very real, be extremely ready and nonchalant about variations of prices.

- Use trustworthy sites and platforms

  Even to check data on cryptocurrencies, ensure that you are using a verified website. Apps and websites can have malware on them, so be completely sure about them before downloading them. Some signs of malware are popup ads popping up all time, your browser is getting redirected, you receive scary warnings and notifications out of nowhere, etc. Laws are forming regularly to control the threats lingering in crypto, but they are not well established as other forms of investment.

- The rumor mill did not work in high school; it will not work here either

The crypto world is surrounded by misinformation. There are multiple sites, hundreds, in fact, that lack credible data. New investors are susceptible to these predatory sites and waste their time on unverified information. Many tips on social media trends, only to be debunked later on. There are also self-styled and designed crypto analyst groups on Facebook, Instagram, and WhatsApp that are filled with accomplices that couch for fake crypto news's accuracy. They trap beginning investors by charging money for tips and giving them bad advice. Always check the news on verified sources. When someone tells you to invest in a coin, look at its market cap and trade rate. If both are down, then obviously do not buy them.

- Use Blue Chips

Just like in any commodity, you have certain blue chips in your markets. Cryptocurrencies also have them, and you should mostly focus on them. It is tempting to put your money on a low-price coin and get a hundred or thousands of them, but their worth will be zero if they disappear. Bigger coins are costly, and you might not be able to fully buy one, but they are more stable. You can buy the coins infractions and get the benefits regardless. The fundamental 'Blue Chip' of cryptocurrency is Bitcoin, and it drives the whole market. Globally recognized coins are used more by the public, and the chances of the price of them being manipulated are low.

Fact

A 'Blue Chip' is a globally recognized, well-established company or entity.

- Taxman wants his cut

  This is an extremely important entity that you cannot just ignore. It is payable on the income you are getting from cryptocurrency trading. There are also fees per transaction you need to look at. Learn more about the tax laws concerning cryptocurrencies and what strategies you need to follow to minimize them, continue reading the next chapter.

Chapter 8: Enter the Taxman…. YES, You Must Pay HIM!

Cryptocurrency has formed its cult of followers, containing thousands of members around the world. It has become an important asset class that cannot be ignored by the government. The popularity of digital currency is ever-growing, but the laws that dictate it are yet to reach with the times. Unfortunately, many laws around it are confusing and complicated. The IRS has answered some important questions and has given some clarity to the subject the past year, but many questions remain unsolved. To avoid calls from the IRS, you need to know everything about cryptocurrency tax laws.

If you understand how cryptocurrencies are taxed, you will know how much you must give the government and avoid paying more than what you owe.

Cryptocurrency Taxes

Cryptocurrency in the United States of America is treated not as a currency but as property. Therefore, you will need to report your capital gains and losses just like you would for real estate, stocks, and bonds. You then have to pay them according to the tax rate at the time. These rates depend upon how long the property was in your ownership and your tax bracket of that year.

Fact

A capital gain occurs when you sell an asset at a higher price than when you got the asset. Capital loss happens when you sell an asset at a lower price than its initial base.

Short-Term Capital Gains Tax

The taxes that apply here are equivalent to income tax rates. You will have to buy and sell your digital within the same year for this to apply. However, these taxes are higher than the rates you get with long-term holders.

Long-Term Capital Gains Tax

If you buy a cryptocurrency coin and hold onto it for longer than one year, these rates apply to you. It needs to be in your possession for over one year before you can sell or exchange it. These rates, as previously mentioned, are lower than what you are charged during short-term gains.

How To Report Them in America?

People can be confused as to what counts as a taxable event and what does not. According to law, there are four types of events that you can partake in as a taxable cryptocurrency investor. These are:

- Selling digital coins for local currency.
- Changing the type of digital currency, for example, Bitcoin for Ethereum, although like-kind exchanges are not allowed.
- Exchanging digital coins for a service or product.
- Getting additional digital coins because of forks, mining, or as an income.

These are the only tasks that are taxable, and other actions you take with your cryptocurrencies are non-taxable. Some popular events are considered taxable by the layman but are non-taxable include:

- Getting crypto coins with local currency.
- Giving crypto coins to a tax-exempt organization like many charities.
- Sending someone crypto coins as gifts with a value less than $15000.

- Transfer crypto coins from one wallet to another, which is also under your name.

Not all cryptocurrency transactions are equal. The different types of transactions mean a different tax law has to be applied. For example, even if you buy a small bagel with your crypto coins from a friend, you are required by the IRS to report the transfer to help them calculate capital gain and loss.

How Are They Taxed?

Calculations are involved in determining total capital gain and loss, which uses data from every transaction you have done with digital coins. You have to know the details of every transaction, how much it cost you when you bought the coins and how much you sold it at the end. You also have to note down fees, commissions, and other charges that you incurred during this time in dollars.

To calculate crypto tax, a simple formula is used. The formula is as follows:

Cost Basis = (Purchase Price in dollars + Fess)/Quantity

For example, if you bought 2 BTC for $19000 and the fees involved were $1000, then your cost basis will be:

Cost Basis = 19,000+1000/2

Cost Basis = 20,000/2

Cost Basis = $10,000

What Details Are Necessary?

For every transaction involving cryptocurrency, you have to note down four important details. These are:

- The time and date when the transaction occurred
- Your basis and the fair market value of the individual coins at the time.
- The date and time of every coin when they were given away. They could be sold, exchanged, and also be disposed of.
- The amount of fiat money, product, or property you receive from each transaction.

The capital gain or loss is found out by using the formula above, in which your cost basis or purchasing price needs to be minus the fair market value of that coin. For example, if you bought a Bitcoin for $1000 and then sold it at a profit of $2000 at the end of the year, then you will have $1000 as a capital gain on the transaction. Depending on whether it is a short-term or a long-term investment, a tax rate is applied. Let's say that the capital tax rate is 15%, then you have to pay $15 on every $100 profit or gain you have made. For $1000, you would have to pay $150.

Fact

You can use the technique FIFO or "first in, first out" accounting to help you keep track of all the coins. In this technique, you label every coin with the date of purchase and start selling the coins that you acquired first. You can also individually specify when every coin that was in ownership by you was bought.

The goal is to report capital gains and losses in such a way that decreases the amount you have to pay. This happens when you report a capital loss. The optimal choice is to decide what to report as a capital loss and capital gain. For example, it is in your best interest to report a capital loss because that decreases the tax bill, and you have to pay less overall.

Laws Around Airdrops and Forks, Are They Taxable?

Fact

Airdrop is a practice in which free crypto coins are distributed to hundreds of wallets. This is a marketing scheme that gains the attention and interest of the public.

It is not normal that forks start with a high valuation. Usually, their value is down because of internal conflicts, but someone might leave you with a malicious fork and airdrop that would increase your tax bill. The coins and tokens that you are dealing with can have higher taxes when you buy them and become lower value when you sell them. You could end up paying a tax on them as well, even though it is a capital loss. These are not uncommon occurrences when you are dealing with digital currencies.

The laws around airdrops and forks have not been straightforward, and many people get confused by them. The IRS has passed new cryptocurrency rules and has given more tax guidance in previous years. However, the new rules are still incomplete and leave many problems unsolved.

Fact

The full form of IRS is the "Internal Revenue Service."
This is a US federal government agency that collects taxes.
The agency was created in the 18th century to overcome the
cost of war at the time.

The new rules have reflected on the treatment of
cryptocurrencies acquired through airdrop and forks. It
states that any coins created and given to you by a hard fork
or an airdrop need to be reported when you are doing your
taxes. It will be treated as an income equal to the fair
market value of the new coin at the time it was given to
you. This is a tax liability. So even if you do not want the
coins, you will still have to pay a tax on them.

Are There Mining Taxes?

As time has passed, cryptocurrency mining has also
become less and less popular. This is because professional
operators and experts have replaced individual miners,
especially for Bitcoin and other higher valuation coins.
However, many individuals mine low-value coins hoping
that they will also rise in price as bitcoin did. These people
are subjected to a tax liability because they can be taxed
twice when mining new coins.

The two types of taxes applied to mining coins are:

- The mined coined will be treated as an income on your tax report with a 0-dollar cost basis. So, for example, if you acquired $100 from mining, you have to pay tax on all $100.
- The trades you will perform with your new coins will incur either a gain or loss. That will also be taxed. So, for example, if you sold your crypto coins from before for $150, you have to pay taxes on the $50 profit you got. This is in addition to the previous income tax.

One way to reduce your tax bill when you are mining coins is that you can repost qualified business expenses. These expenses occurring during the mining operation can make your tax significantly lowered. For example, the computer and hardware you have used to mine crypto coins can deduct your tax costs.

Mistakes Involving Cryptocurrencies Tax Calculations

- Report Full History

  Be sure to include transaction events with cryptocurrencies of past years. Many people assume that they only have to report or inform the IRS of the activities regarding crypto of one recent year when filing for annual taxes. That is the common-sense approach to it. You might think they already know about your previous activities from last year's tax files, but that is not the case.

It is quite jarring to know that you have to write down your entire cryptocurrency trading history when filing for cryptocurrency taxes. This is because of a concept called "Basis Value."

The cost basis is the initial price of the commodity, which is paid by the current owner to the previous owner. Because crypto coins go through extreme volatility in price, it is difficult to figure out the initial or cost basis. The only way to accurately identify the cost basis is to attach all the previous trading history in your tax files. If you do not, then your reports will be invalid or incomplete.

If you have not recorded them for a long time, you can use tax encryption software to help you with your calculations. Fortunately, because of this, you can save a lot of money on your taxes by showing your previous capital losses.

- Do not ignore the losses

Whenever you turn a profit with crypto trading, you will be taxed. But, if you report a loss with crypto trading, that can decrease the amount you have to pay. Unfortunately, beginners often make the mistake of not writing down their losses, saving them a ton of money. Unfortunately, this is very common as taxpayers do not know what techniques and methods can be used to reduce the taxable amount you get from capital gains.

Because crypto coins are treated as property rather than currency, their losses work just like property losses as well. That means that if you have any loss on crypto trading within a year, then you can use them to compensate for capital gains and get a lower figure on your tax.

Not only can you compensate for capital gain and reduce the, but you can also use the losses to offset up to $3000 on your general income tax.

Another thing you can do to reduce your tax is to sell your coin at a loss on December 31st and then buy it back on January 1st. As of today, the Wash Sale Rule does not apply to crypto, so you can use this technique to show losses on your tax report.

- Using Inconsistent Methods

One of the most effective and common cost basis methods is FIFO. It is when you sell coins in the order in which they are bought. This method is highly advised, and it is also the default calculation that many people use.

However, there are different methods to calculate cost basis, and you can also use the Last IN First Out method. As the name suggests, the last coin is the first one to be sold by the investor. There are other methods as well, and all of them effectively help you with your cryptocurrency taxes. However, they can lead to different outcomes when calculating your overall tax figure.

Therefore, the investor or individual crypto traders decide the choice for cost basis according to their preference. But as you start to use one, you are then stuck with it. The IRS does not encourage you to use a different method than you have used previously. If you have found out that you do not like your current method after a year or two, you must send a physical copy of the request to ask permission from the IRS to change it. There is no proper timing as to when they will answer back, not even a guarantee that they will accept your request.

You can change the method of collecting your data after some time, but it can be tedious. You could use any method, and the task will still feel tiring. This mandatory request can lead to many potential failures as well. Some people do not have the time to calculate and file tax reports and hit down details of every transaction. For them, accounting professionals who are experts in cryptocurrencies and taxes revolving around cryptocurrencies can help. It will also be a good decision to use professional accountants or tax firms that work with crypto.

Cryptocurrencies are on the rise and, by the looks of it, will keep on rising. Thus, they have become an important class of assets, and many individuals who are investing in them, do not know much about their tax laws. If you read them yourself, you might get lost in technical jargon. Always keep a lookout for more guidance released from the IRS on the subject so you will be up to date with everything. Any cryptocurrency holder should also ensure that they are using correct software for their cryptocurrencies tax calculation, including capital gain and loss figures. It is also advisable that you seek advice from professional accounts on this subject to make sure everything is done right.

How to Use Your Losses in Tax Gains?

If you have ever experienced a loss, you would know that it is one of the most gut-wrenching feelings you can experience. All your hard work feels worthless. However, smart investors in crypto have figured out a way to turn their losses into gains by offsetting crypto capital gains in their portfolios.

Fact

Cryptocurrency investors have been given a nickname in the finance world and are sometimes referred to as "buy and hodl" investors. "Hodl" is an acronym for the phrase "hold on for dear life" because cryptocurrency investing is a risky endeavor.

The strategy they use is tax-loss harvesting. You can use it to your advantage when investing in cryptocurrencies. The strategy works because of unique rules governing digital coins.

Tax Loss Harvesting

This is the practice of selling assets or commodities that have decreases in price and value to claim a loss on your tax files. Once you claim the loss, you can decrease your tax figure significantly. You can apply this technique each year as well. Using this technique at the right times can increase after-tax annual returns by 0.25% each year.

After you realize a loss or incur a loss, then you can buy a similar asset to maintain an optimal asset allocation. It is a nifty technique, but IRS Section 1091 states prevent purchasing an identical asset within 30 days after a sale. This rule was implemented because the government wanted transactions to have real economic value rather than only be done for tax purposes.

To overcome this IRS rule, the general investor and stock market enthusiast purchases different equities and indexes. They will have the same risks involved and similar return characteristics, but because they will be composed of different companies and security holdings, they will not be targeted by the IRS.

Tax Loss Harvesting with Cryptocurrencies

This IRS rule applies to shares of stocks and securities" as it is written in section 1091. However, the IRS also has treated cryptocurrencies as property and not stock or securities. This makes tax-loss harvesting with crypto much easier than other assets because rules do not apply to it.

You can sell all your crypto and then buy it back only to harvest loss as a crypto investor. You can also decrease your income tax bill. Because of this loophole, many aggressive investors go overboard and avoid paying taxes on their crypto gains, which is why the rule was put in the first place for other assets.

You can save many hard-earned dollars on this strategy, but you should not try to abuse it. The IRS can detect and argue that you have done an immediate transaction that does not help the economy. Therefore, no offset should be given to you. Even if the IRS loses this fight, the cost of going to court is not worth it.

The Best Strategy

To avoid getting into Thebes of the IRS, you have to sell a crypto coin into a highly correlated Intermediate currency before buying your original currency back. This way, there will be a time gap and also a layer of the transaction between the sale and repurchase. It will be in your best interest to space out the transactions so that the regulators see the economic value. As an informed investor, you should always keep looking at the news for changes in this rule as well.

Also, hold growing crypto coins for more than a year and do not sell them immediately. Tax rates on long-term gains are lower, as discussed above.

Always add information about crypto losses and take advantage of tax-loss harvesting.

There are also crypto IRAs available that can be used to make tax-deductible contributions, and you will only need to pay tax when you take the coins out of this IRA.

Now that you know how to make money off of crypto and the laws surrounding it, you can learn what to do with the money you have earned.

Chapter 9: What to Do with The Money I Made?

You have now learned how to financially benefit from the crypto craze that has been affecting the world. You know where to buy, research and safely store them. You have also learned the various laws affecting the crypto sphere. However, you will need to withdraw the coins after a while at some point in your life.

After acquiring some bitcoin and other cryptocurrencies for yourself, you need to be able to turn them into cash with ease. If you have some digital coins, you might be tempted to 'sell' them and get the money transferred directly into your bank, or you may want to convert your coins into cash without involving unnecessary third-party. Either way, to buy and use your earned money, you need to turn your digital assets into local currency. There are many ways to do this, each of them requiring unique steps. Here are some of the most common ways to convert crypto into government-backed fiat currency.

Consideration Before Cashing Out Your Coins

You need to know certain factors before you transfer coins into your bank. These factors are:

Taxes:

As previously mentioned, you need to mention to the IRS if you have made a profit by buying and selling bitcoin, and that tax will come on your profit income. Have this in the back of your head when filing up for taxes the next year. Suppose you are using a reputable third-party broker exchange. In that case, they usually report their transactions to the government so remember to do your taxes properly.

Fees:

When you transfer your digital coins into local cash or your bank account, the process will likely cost you some extra charges.

Speed:

Depending on the method you choose and the third-party broker exchange you use, it can take a couple of days to transfer your money into your bank.

Methods of Cashing Out

The most popular way to convert your coins into local money and put them into your local bank account.

Why Exchange Your Coins for Bank Balance?

The main reason for purchasing digital coins and investing in cryptocurrency is to ultimately make a profit by turning them into local currency. Just like you, hundreds of people around the world are buying Ethereum and Bitcoin because they see them as an asset or commodity that will grow in price with time. Therefore, you hold your coins because you believe that they will increase in value later. However, like in every industry, the value of crypto coins also decreases, and since the demand for them has increased in recent years, you might be able to make a profit if you sell your coins now and take equivalent cash in your bank account.

The popularity of cryptocurrencies is growing, but it is still lacking the stability and acceptability that local currencies have. Where there is a chance of a store denying your coins as payment, no store will deny your credit card backed by local cash. You will be able to buy anything from anywhere.

Also, the reason why we are investing in crypto is that we want profits out of its growth. Those profits can only be truly appreciated when you convert your crypto coins into local money. There is always a chance that prices might decrease in the market, so putting your profits in a safe place is a smart choice.

How To Move Coins to A Bank Account?

Whenever you fly into a new country that uses a different currency, you go through a simple process to convert your money into that currency, usually at the airport itself. Think of changing crypto money into local cash in the same way. You are essentially 'selling' your coins and 'buying' dollars at equal value. You have the option of turning your coins into not only dollars or other currencies of your choice.

The amount you will be getting for your crypto is called an exchange rate. The exchange rate of local currencies is determined by how that currency's countries are economically faring and the actions of that country's government. In the crypto world, there is no central authority. The 'exchange rates' of coins are decided by their demand in the market.

The amount of money you will get from your coins is determined by how many people want to buy that digital coin and how much they are willing to give you.

Transferring your digital coins into a bank account is similar to exchanging currencies. But because they have no central authority, the entire process of coins being exchanged is kept private. Therefore, it does not matter what your country's economic conditions are or what state it is in.

The first method is to use a third-party exchange broker. These brokers will provide a rate according to the market prices of your coins at the time and will exchange them for you. Their processing is secure, and it only takes a few simple steps.

The second method is called a P2P transaction or peer-to-peer transaction. This technique of converting your coins into cash is more private and anonymous. In addition, because you sell your coins directly to a person, that means it is also faster.

Cashing Out Using a Broker Exchange

A broker exchange is one of the easiest and simplest ways you can cash out your coins. Here are the general steps that you will need to follow:

- Decide which third-party broker you are going to use. For example, you can use an exchange that you have already used to buy and/or store crypto coins.
- If it is an exchange broker that you have never used, sign up and create an account by completing the verification process.
- Put or buy digital coins in your account.
- Enter your withdrawal information in the account which will include your bank account or PayPal account details.
- Now, you are all set to withdraw the amount that you want. The withdrawal may have a certain limit. It can also take 4-6 days till the money reaches your bank account. Some transaction fees will be deducted at this step.

Third-Party Broker Exchanges

Cryptocurrency exchanges are not a new entity but simply another name for cryptocurrency exchanges that we have learned about in previous chapters. The process of changing your coins shows resemblance to the process of changing money in a foreign currency at an airport. First, you have to store or deposit your coins into the exchange. After they have received your digital coins, you can go into their menu and request a withdrawal. A withdrawal usually can be made in any currency of your choosing at most exchanges. You may need to provide your bank account details so that the money is withdrawn directly into your account.

Brokers and exchanges are strictly regulated by laws and regulations, as they should be, especially being monitored for money laundering laws. For this reason, you can only provide one bank account for withdrawal purposes.

This method can be very simple, secure, and easy, but you have to take into account speed. It is not the fastest method. It will take about one week for your money to reach your bank account, and it is also affected by what country you live in. Extra charges can be fined as well, depending on which country your bank is situated in.

There are also bitcoin ATMs and Debit cards that work only for bitcoin that work similarly to third-party brokers. In both exchanges and debit cards, you will need to upload or store your coins in an account. Then, you will sell those coins to get physical cash. Unfortunately, this feature cannot be used for other cryptocurrencies and has high transaction fees associated with it.

The popular broker exchanges you can work with include Coinbase and Kraken. You can do more than just buy and sell crypto coins on these sites because they offer a multitude of services.

P2P / Peer-to-Peer Services

Suppose you want your transfers to occur quickly and more anonymously. In that case, you can use this method to sell your digital currency for local money. You can ask your buyer to transfer the money in any currency and bank account you want using the payment method that you are most comfortable with. This system allows for quicker transfers, and you will not pay excessive fees. A third-party broker is often set on the rate at which they are going to buy your count. However, an individual buyer can give you more than these brokers offer for the same amount of coins.

The buyer can deposit your money directly into your bank or use international payment services such as Paypal. Wait for them to send you proof of ID and proof of transfer before sending your coins to them.

Some people might say that peer-to-peer selling is too dangerous for the risk, but it is very safe. You just need to know what you are doing. Fraudsters exist everywhere, and you need to be aware of them. A good idea would be to use a peer-to-peer payment platform that keeps your coins locked until the buyer confirms the payment and you until you have received the notification of that payment.

Fact

One of the most popular peer-to-peer platforms for exchanging coins is LocalBitcoins.

Cashing Out Using a Peer-to-Peer Exchange

You will have to follow a few simple steps to use P2P exchange to turn your digital sound into local currency. The steps are as follows:

- Choose the peer-to-peer exchange platform to work with. There are many popular choices out there that are tried and tested. LocalBitcoin, LocalEthereum are some examples of them.

- Make a new account by signing up to the platform or site. While signing up, you will be asked to choose a location for the buyer.

- Use the marketplace to make contact with potential buyers and offer them a trade. Many people are looking to buy crypto, so this will not be a hard task.

- Many peer-to-peer sites have an option where you can store your coins until you have confirmed that payment has been made. Once you have confirmed it, the coins are released to the buyer.

Fact

The legal arrangement in which a third individual or party holds a large sum of money until a condition is met in trade – called an escrow. This is done mostly in the housing market, where the buyer and seller both are protected from fraud.

To simplify the process, many peer to power platforms have advertisement capabilities where you can publish and add more coins. However, this method might involve extra charges. Suppose you are uncomfortable selecting a buyer by yourself. In that case, you can use rating sites such as eBay to see previous feedback of a potential buyer. If they have a good record, then you can be more confident with the sale.

P2P platforms are used mainly by people who want their transactions to be private. So, to make it more anonymous, many people use VPNs to secure their internet. You might want to use payment methods such as web money and gift vouchers as well.

Exchange Broker or Peer to Peer

You can now pay for your day-to-day bills and junk food requirements by turning your digital coins into paper money. However, you may only want to turn them into cash because you see that this asset has made a profit or the market is going unstable. If you are a beginner, then using a third-party broker will be more convenient and safer. But, if you have gained some experience and want to get a higher price for your coins than the market, use peer-to-peer platforms.

Cashing Out Using Coinbase

Coinbase is one of the most popular broker exchanges out there. There is no limit to withdrawal on Coinbase, so you can withdraw as much cash as you want using this site. To cash out your funds using Coinbase, you need to follow these steps:

- The first step is to sell your cryptocurrency for cash.
- Click the Buy/Sell option on the Coinbase Site or Coinbase mobile app.
- Tap on 'Sell.'
- Now, click on the crypto coins you want to sell.
- Enter the number of coins you want to sell in the blank space provided.
- Select Preview sell and then Sell Now to complete the process.

You have now sold your coins for cash, which will be available in your local currency wallet. This local currency wallet can be in USD, Euro, Pounds, etc. This process can be done in mere minutes by using the Coinbase mobile app or Coinbase site.

The second step is to withdraw the money. Using a web browser:

- Select 'Assets.'
- Select the cash balance you want to take out.
- The Cash-Out tab will open. Enter the amount you want to withdraw in the blank space provided.
- Select 'Continue.'
- Now choose your preferred location for cash out.
- Select 'Continue.'
- Finally, select Cash Out to complete your transfer.

If you are using the mobile app, then:

- You only need to click 'Cash Out.'
- In the blank space provided enter the amount you want to withdraw and choose the destination of withdrawal.
- Click 'Preview Cash Out.'
- And then click 'Cash Out' to complete your transaction.

Cashing out using LocalBitcoins

One of the most popular peer-to-peer platforms for selling bitcoin is LocalBitcoin. However, to turn your money into cash and be able to withdraw, you have to follow these steps:

1. First, you will need to set up an account on LocalBitcoin by signing up. To create the account, you will need to enter a username and a password. Make sure to use a strong password with characters. You will also provide an email address.
2. Now, you will be logged in. When you are logged in, click on the Sell Bitcoin icon on the top of the browser.
3. Now, you will need to select a country from which you will choose a buyer. Choose a country where ideal buyers are located. You can also choose your own country, but this is not necessary. Even if you live in Brazil, you can select the US or the UK to attract buyers.
4. Next, you will select the number of coins you wish to sell. Then, you can sell your coins and have the money transferred to your local bank or online banks.
5. Now, select a buyer. When you spot a potential buyer, their transaction history and feedback will be displayed on their profile. For example, someone with 90-100% positive feedback will be a good choice. You can also see how many trades they have completed. For example, if they have traded over 200 times, chances are they are a serious, legitimate buyer.
6. Reconfirm how many bitcoins you want to sell.

7. If you have selected to withdraw money from your local bank, you will have to provide your bank's account number. If you have selected Paypal as your withdrawal address, then you have to enter your PayPal email address.

8. Finally, you have to select 'Send Trade.'

9. Now, you will have to wait. Your buyer will receive a notification of your request. Then, they will have to see and accept your request.

10. You will then send your bitcoins into the LocalBitcoin escrow system and wait for the buyer to pay you using your chosen payment.

11. Once you have received the payment, confirm it in your Local Bitcoins account and release your coins to the buyer.

12. The buyer will directly contact you when he/she has sent the money, and then you can use your bank's app or site to check for it.

The process takes a little more time than broker exchanges, and it can be a little daunting at first, but with more experience, you will get comfortable. You can choose a different payment method every time you want to sell, and the most beneficial thing about local bitcoin is that you can sell your coins at a higher price than the market value.

If you think that no one is accepting your request, then it is also a good time to use advertising to help you sell your coins. The ads will cost 1% in fees, but you can get a buyer sooner that agrees with your price and payment method. In addition, the ads will pop up in the accounts of potential buyers, and you will get a notification if one of them is interested in your offer.

Word of Caution

LocalBitcoin is the only one in the sea of P2P platforms that you can choose from. There are many others where you can trade other cryptocurrencies. The important thing is to always check that the platform you are using has an escrow payment system. Also, never send your coins before you receive payment from a potential buyer.

Cashing Out Small Amounts

It will be a hectic day if you ever need to withdraw your entire savings. Logistically, it will be a nightmare, and such a rare anomaly would most certainly be investigated by higher authorities. Such withdrawals create suspicion, and you want to avoid them. The best way to withdraw your amount is to do so in small amounts. You can only take the amount you need every 1st of the month.

Here are a few ways you can achieve this:

- Sell your coins, equivalent to only the small amount that you need, from an exchange broker to your local bank or use peer-to-peer exchanges like LocalBitcoin or Local Ethereum.

- You can also use payment processors that directly send cryptocurrency to bank accounts for bills, rent, fees, and income. You can skip sending all your money to an account and let a company do it for you. Examples of some payment processors are CoinPayments, SpectroCoin, SpicePay, etc.

- You get yourself and also your employees a prepaid Visa or Mastercard that can be topped with cryptocurrency. This card can be used to pay online and offline at stores with POS (point of sale) machines. For example, you can get them at Monaco, TenX, etc.

- You can cash out small amounts by directly paying your employees or service providers with cryptocurrency. You can tell them how to withdraw them and how to change them into fiat. To use this method, you need to first find a service provider that agrees to this payment method first.

Cashing Out Big Amounts

Unfortunately, there is no one-step solution to cashing out a big amount using cryptocurrency. However, people at

Bitwala are currently in the process of building a platform that merges the crypto and banking experience so that you can get more services with your ICO investments.

Fact

ICO stands for Initial coin offering.

Conclusion

Cryptocurrency or crypto has become a buzzword because it has shown the world that it has the potential to make extreme profits for you. Normal individuals, just like you and me, invested a few hundred dollars in them only 5 or 10 years ago, and now they are living their dreams. Some of us will have to work every day for the rest of our lives, in stress taking jobs only to achieve a minuscule amount of profits compared to their success.

There is a community of people dedicated to helping you achieve profits just as they have. The crypto society is filled with enthusiastic and informed individuals that can guide you in times of confusion. Although everything you need to know is covered in this book.

You have learned what started the cryptocurrency trend and why it is likely to grow even more in the upcoming years. You have learned the major contenders in the industry and found out how they worked. You are not the only one interested in crypto and blockchain technology, as hundreds of companies have adopted this technology themselves in their new projects. After reading, now you know where to buy and store your crypto coins safely and efficiently. You also have an idea of the laws and regulations surrounding crypto coins and crypto investing and learn the best method to follow them along with making profits.

The future of cryptocurrencies looks bright, and there is a chance that you might miss out on making it big. Do not let that happen. Many people say that they will invest and work on their finances. Still, because of anxiety or laziness, they stay where they are. I want you to become successful in life so that you and your families may become financially stable. Now that you know about all the steps to take, now is your choice to take them.

Going through this journey, you will feel overwhelmed and anxious. You might make bad decisions by letting greed and fear take over your thought process. Do not let that happen either. Your mental health is one of your most important assets. Take care of it as you cannot live without a calm mind. Never invest any amount that you are not ready to lose. Have a family member, friend, or roommate help you whenever you are not feeling fine. I have a facebook group that has helped many people. They have been where you are now. Join the Investing on a Budget Facebook group. In the group we help each other and hear of each other's journeys.

It can be that the first time you invest, you might not get the profits you desire. That is normal. Every industry goes through crests and troughs; cryptocurrency is no exception. If the industry is going down, know that the rose always occurs after it. You need to keep trying because as the market explodes just as it had in the past decade, you will see success unlike ever before. I look forward to hearing from you. Leave a review on Amazon or wherever you bought the book. I want to make sure the information is clear and concise and I can't do that without your input.

Getting into cryptocurrencies might be a new thing for you, but everything you do it at some time. Therefore, there is no reason to be hesitant because something is new. To make your life better, physically, mentally, and financially, you have to keep trying new activities and going to new places. Such a mindset will make your mind and body fresh, and you will live a much more interesting and fulfilling life. It is better to try what you want to achieve than be regretful 50 years later when you are at your life's end.

New activities, goals, and skills are what makes an individual more skillful and knowledgeable. Even if you do not want to learn a new skill, you must know why and how people around you are interested in it. Being well informed and educated about the world you live in will make you more ready for taking opportunities at the right time. You will be one step ahead of your peers in finding out solutions and taking chances that they might have missed. Being more learned can only bring you more confidence, friends, and money.

Now that you have learned about crypto and what this industry offers, teach it to other individuals who have no clue about this famous industry. Tell them how it works and about the opportunities that it can give. Then, spend some time with them or even recommend this book. Being helpful to others is a good way to stay mindful and happy.

Every human who had ever lived had once dreamed of doing something. Most of them never had an opportunity to do anything about it. The dream that you want to be able to not worry about money and live a fulfilling life is standing right in front of you. The opportunity that cryptocurrency has given to the public does not come often. Take this book to act as the time is right to get into the industry. Achieve your dreams, pass your financial goals, make your family happy and safe.

Your family and friends are the people that care about you the most, and you need to cherish them just the same. To want to be rich or financially stable is a noble goal that suggests that you care about your loved ones. You want your children to go to college and you and your partner to have a good retirement. You want to give something back to your parents for taking care of you.

I hope that you live a happy and healthy life filled with success and profits. I hope that this book has provided you with every information you have been looking for and has motivated you to start changing your life for the better. If this book has helped you in any way, leave a review and even share the book, among others. Here is my personal email address should you have any questions or concerns mcarter@legendaryproductsandservices.com.

I wish you good luck on your crypto investing journey.

Index

USD coin, 42

References

1. *About Publication 544, Sales and Other Dispositions of Assets | Internal Revenue Service.* (n.d.). Internal Revenue Service. https://www.irs.gov/forms-pubs/about-publication-544

2. *Accept Bitcoin and Crypto Payments.* (n.d.). SpectroCoin. https://spectrocoin.com/en/accept-bitcoin-payments.html

3. Akerlof, G. A., & Shiller, R. J. (2019, May 21). *How 'animal spirits' destabilize economies.* McKinsey & Company. https://www.mckinsey.com/featured-insights/employment-and-growth/how-animal-spirits-destabilize-economies

4. *As an investor in cryptocurrency, how often do you check the crypto market?* (n.d.). Quora. https://www.quora.com/As-an-investor-in-crypto currency-how-often-do-you-check-the-crypto-mar ket

5. B. (2019a, January 26). *ICO - Initial Coin Offering - BitcoinWiki*. BitcoinWiki. https://en.bitcoinwiki.org/wiki/ICO_(Initial_Coi n_Offering)

6. B., B., B., B., & B. (2019b, March 6). *Video Guide: What is Hashing?* Blockgeeks. http://blockgeeks.com/guides/video-guide-what-i s-hashing/

7. Banks Editorial Team. (2021, July 23). *Learn How To Convert Bitcoin To Cash*. Banks.Com. https://www.banks.com/articles/investing/crypto currency/convert-bitcoin-cash/

8. BBC News. (2018, January 25). *50 Cent forgot he had a stash of Bitcoin now worth $8m.* https://www.bbc.com/news/business-42820246

9. *Best Bitcoin Wallets of 2021.* (2021, November 9). Investopedia. https://www.investopedia.com/best-bitcoin-walle ts-5070283

10. *Best Blockchain Stocks to Buy.* (n.d.). Money. https://money.usnews.com/investing/stock-mark et-news/slideshows/best-blockchain-stocks-to-bu y

11. *Best Crypto Exchanges.* (2021, November 8). Investopedia. https://www.investopedia.com/best-crypto-excha nges-5071855

12. Bigmore, R. (2018, May 25). *A decade of cryptocurrency: from bitcoin to mining chips.* The

Telegraph.
https://www.telegraph.co.uk/technology/digital-money/the-history-of-cryptocurrency/

13. *Bitcoin (BTC) Price, Charts, and News | Coinbase: bitcoin price, btc price, bitcoin coinbase.* (2021, December 1). Coinbase.
https://www.coinbase.com/price/bitcoin

14. *Bitcoin Cash (BCH) Price, Charts, and News | Coinbase: bitcoin cash price, bitcoin cash, bitcoin price.* (2021a, November 11). Coinbase.
https://www.coinbase.com/price/bitcoin-cash

15. *Bitcoin Cash (BCH) Price, Charts, and News | Coinbase: bitcoin cash price, bitcoin cash, bitcoin price.* (2021b, November 11). Coinbase.
https://www.coinbase.com/price/bitcoin-cash

16. *Bitwala - Nuri.* (n.d.). Nuri.
https://nuri.com/bank/

17. *Blockchain Explained.* (2021, November 4).

Investopedia.

https://www.investopedia.com/terms/b/blockchai

n.asp

18. *Bloomberg - Are you a robot?* (n.d.). Bloomberg.

https://www.bloomberg.com/tosv2.html?vid=&uu

id=a1c7dec5-52fc-11ec-9bbe-504c71546677&url=L

25ld3MvYXJoaWNsZXMvMjAxOCowNy0xOS9jc

nlwdG8taGVpc3QtaW5zdXJhbmNlLWZhdC1wcm

VtaXVtcy1sb3RzLW9mLXVuZGVyd3JpdGluZy1ya

XNr

19. Bobsguide. (2021, May 13). *Why are there so*

many cryptocurrencies?

https://www.bobsguide.com/articles/why-are-the

re-so-many-cryptocurrencies

20. *Buy & Sell Crypto On The LocalCryptos P2P Marketplace*. (n.d.). LocalCryptos. https://localcryptos.com/

21. *Buying & Selling*. (2019, June 6). Investopedia. https://www.investopedia.com/buying-and-sellin g-4689764

22. C. (2021, September 16). *Funding for beginners*. Coin Telegraph. https://cointelegraph.com/funding-for-beginners

23. *Can Bitcoin Be Hacked?* (2021, July 26). Investopedia. https://www.investopedia.com/articles/investing/ 032615/can-bitcoin-be-hacked.asp

24. *The Capital Gains Tax and How to Calculate It*. (2021, September 7). Investopedia. https://www.investopedia.com/terms/c/capital_g ains_tax.asp

25. Capital, P. (n.d.). *Personal Capital*. Personal Capital. https://www.personalcapital.com/get-started?ircli ckid=2JizoX1T6xyIR811SZ0S0yHbUkG28j3Jj3zd VY0&impact_partner=WebPals%20Systems%20S .C.%20Ltd.&impact_partnerID=71682&utm_sour ce=WebPals%20Systems%20S.C.%20Ltd.&utm_ medium=affiliate&irgwc=1&partner=investorJunk ie

26. Cash, M. (2020, February 21). *Why are there so many cryptocurrencies in the market? | Mercury Cash Blog*. Mercury Cash Blog |. https://blog.mercury.cash/2020/02/14/why-are-t here-so-many-cryptocurrencies-in-the-market/

27. Claeys, B. (2021, December 1). *CryptoMiso - Ranking cryptocurrencies based on Github*

commits. CryptoMiso.

https://www.cryptomiso.com/

28. *Coin Payments*. (n.d.). Coin Payments.

https://www.coinpayments.net/

29. *Coinbase*. (n.d.). Investor Junkie.

https://investorjunkie.com/wp-json/xm-link/coin

base?p=80716

30. CoinGecko. (n.d.). *Cryptocurrency Prices, Charts,*

and Crypto Market Cap.

https://www.coingecko.com/en

31. *CoinMarketCal*. (n.d.). CoinMarketCal.

https://coinmarketcal.com/en/

32. Cointelegraph. (2021, October 19). *What is Bitcoin*

blockchain? A guide to the technology behind

BTC.

https://cointelegraph.com/bitcoin-for-beginners/

how-does-blockchain-work-a-beginners-guide-to-blockchain-technology

33. *Community-driven Bitcoin Statistics and Services.* (n.d.). Coin Dance. https://coin.dance/

34. Corporate Finance Institute. (2021, February 3). *Fiat Money.* https://corporatefinanceinstitute.com/resources/knowledge/economics/fiat-money-currency/

35. *Crypto Withdrawals - General Information.* (n.d.). Crypto.Com Help Center. https://help.crypto.com/en/articles/2500695-crypto-withdrawals-general-information

36. *Cryptocurrencies & Bitcoin History : How it all Began.* (2021, November 10). Ledger. https://www.ledger.com/academy/crypto/a-brief-history-on-bitcoin-cryptocurrencies

37. *Cryptocurrency Tax: How Is Cryptocurrency Taxed? | ZenLedger.* (2021, November 3). Zen Ledger. https://www.zenledger.io/blog/how-is-cryptocurrency-taxed?utm_source=Google_ads&utm_medium=paid&utm_campaign=blog&utm_campaign=11912382656&utm_source=google&utm_medium=cpc&utm_content=491838509656&utm_term=cryptocurrency%20taxes&adgroupid=117302959884&gclid=CjoKCQjwm9yJBhDTARIsABKIcGY5i3hu32I9GwEkpCR2AOKndybq_BovYLSp6aArjmqTsqQMYoUokQIaAkPzEALw_wcB

38. Darlington, N., Mitra, R., Rosic, A., Rosic, A., Rosic, A., & Rosic, A. (2021, November 25). *Blockchain For Beginners: What Is Blockchain Technology? A Step-by-Step Guide.* Blockgeeks.

http://blockgeeks.com/guides/what-is-blockchain
-technology/

39. *Digital Assets | Investor.gov.* (n.d.). Investor.

https://www.investor.gov/additional-resources/sp

otlight/spotlight-initial-coin-offerings-and-digital-

assets?utm_source=google&utm_medium=cpc&u

tm_campaign=dae&utm_content=search&gclid=

CjoKCQjw-NaJBhDsARIsAAja6dNwobYzRHBJ-rJ

YKvSc7OonyKdgeSOuQzXsEyl_1_nOojf3WaCuAC

4aAhMsEALw_wcB

40. Disparte, D. A. (2018a, April 16). *In A Real War
Can Virtual Assets Be A Haven?* Forbes.

https://www.forbes.com/sites/dantedisparte/201

8/04/15/in-a-real-war-can-virtual-assets-be-a-hav

en/#35c2abea2a96

41. Disparte, D. A. (2018b, July 21). *Beware Of Crypto
Risks - 10 Risks To Watch.* Forbes.

https://www.forbes.com/sites/dantedisparte/201 8/07/21/beware-of-crypto-risks-10-risks-to-watch /?sh=60577c605f17

42. *Earn crypto while learning about crypto.* (n.d.-a). Coinbase. https://www.coinbase.com/earn

43. *Earn crypto while learning about crypto.* (n.d.-b). Coinbase. https://www.coinbase.com/earn

44. *Ethereum Classic (ETC) Price, Charts, and News | Coinbase: etc price, ethereum classic price, ethereum classic.* (2021, November 11). Coinbase. https://www.coinbase.com/price/ethereum-classi c

45. *Ethereum (ETH) Price, Charts, and News | Coinbase: ethereum price, eth price, ethereum.* (2021, December 1). Coinbase. https://www.coinbase.com/price/ethereum

46. *eToro*. (n.d.). Investor Junkie.

   https://investorjunkie.com/wp-json/xm-link/etor

   o?p=80716

47. ExpressVPN. (n.d.). *ExpressVPN - A Fast and*

   Secure VPN.

   https://www.expressvpn.com/unrestricted-1?p=8

   0716

48. *Financial Institution (FI) Definition with*

   Examples. (2021, April 24). Investopedia.

   https://www.investopedia.com/terms/f/financiali

   nstitution.asp

49. *Foreign Account Tax Compliance Act (FATCA).*

   (2021, November 25). Investopedia.

   https://www.investopedia.com/terms/f/foreign-a

   ccount-tax-compliance-act-fatca.asp

50. Frankel, M. C. (2021, October 25). *7 Blockchain*

   Stocks to Invest In. The Motley Fool.

https://www.fool.com/investing/stock-market/market-sectors/financials/blockchain-stocks/

51. *Gemini.* (n.d.). Investor Junkie.
https://investorjunkie.com/wp-json/xm-link/gemini?p=80716

52. *Glassnode - On-chain market intelligence.* (n.d.).
Glassnode. https://glassnode.com/

53. GOBankingRates. (2009, February 5). *What Are Market Trends?*
https://www.gobankingrates.com/investing/strategy/what-market-trends/

54. GOBankingRates. (2021a, May 11). *Bitcoin (BTC)? What It Is, What It's Worth and Should You Be Investing?*
https://www.gobankingrates.com/investing/crypto/how-to-make-money-with-bitcoin/

55. GOBankingRates. (2021b, June 7). *What Is Market Cap?*
https://www.gobankingrates.com/investing/stocks/what-is-market-cap/

56. GOBankingRates. (2021c, September 30). *What Is Blockchain Technology?*
https://www.gobankingrates.com/investing/crypto/what-is-blockchain-technology/

57. GOBankingRates. (2021d, October 29). *How Much Is Twitter Worth?*
https://www.gobankingrates.com/money/business/how-much-is-twitter-worth/

58. GOBankingRates. (2021e, November 3). *How Much Is Facebook Worth?*
https://www.gobankingrates.com/money/business/how-much-is-facebook-worth/

59. GOBankingRates. (2021f, November 4). *Binance Fees: A Full Breakdown and How It Compares.* https://www.gobankingrates.com/investing/crypt o/binance-fees/

60. GOBankingRates. (2021g, November 15). *10 Best Crypto Research Tools You Must Have as an Investor.* https://www.gobankingrates.com/investing/crypt o/best-crypto-research-tools/

61. GOBankingRates. (2021h, November 15). *Where Does Cryptocurrency Come From?* https://www.gobankingrates.com/investing/crypt o/economy-explained-where-does-cryptocurrency -come-from/

62. Gogol, F. (2021, November 28). *THIS is how to quickly and easily turn your Bitcoin into cash [2021].* Stilt Blog.

https://www.stilt.com/blog/2021/03/how-to-turn
-bitcoin-into-cash/

63. Gordon, S. (2021, March 23). *What is Ripple?*
Bitcoin Magazine: Bitcoin News, Articles, Charts,
and Guides.
https://bitcoinmagazine.com/guides/what-is-ripp
le

64. Hatzakis, S. (2021, November 24). *Best Bitcoin
Brokers 2021.* ForexBrokers.Com.
https://www.forexbrokers.com/guides/best-crypt
ocurrency-brokers

65. *How can I make my account more secure?* |
Coinbase Help. (n.d.). Coinbase.
https://help.coinbase.com/en/coinbase/privacy-a
nd-security/data-privacy/how-can-i-make-my-acc
ount-more-secure.html

66. *How do I cash out my funds? | Coinbase Help.* (n.d.). Coinbase. https://help.coinbase.com/en/coinbase/trading-and-funding/buying-selling-or-converting-crypto/how-do-i-sell-or-cash-out-my-digital-currency

67. *How Many Bitcoins Are There? (Circulating Supply - Live).* (n.d.). Buy Bitcoin Worldwide. https://www.buybitcoinworldwide.com/how-many-bitcoins-are-there/

68. *how often do you check btc prices?* (2017, November 21). Reddit. https://www.reddit.com/r/Bitcoin/comments/7el9yf/how_often_do_you_check_btc_prices/

69. *How often should you check cryptocurrency market | executium Trading System.* (n.d.). Executium. https://executium.com/crypto-currencies/342629

-how-often-should-you-check-cryptocurrency-market/

70. *How the Consortium Blockchain Works.* (2019, September 25). Intellectsoft Blockchain Lab. https://blockchain.intellectsoft.net/blog/how-the-consortium-blockchain-works/

71. *How to invest in cryptocurrency.* (2021, July 1). MarketWatch. http://www.marketwatch.com/picks/what-you-need-to-know-to-start-investing-in-cryptocurrency-right-now-11623683145?tesla=y

72. *How to Sell Bitcoin.* (n.d.). Investor Junkie. https://investorjunkie.com/crypto/how-to-sell-bitcoin/

73. *Internal Revenue Service.* (n.d.). Internal Revenue Service. https://www.irs.gov/individuals/international-tax

payers/frequently-asked-questions-on-virtual-curr
ency-transactions

74. *Introduction to the Bitcoin Wallet.* (2021, August
9). Investopedia.
https://www.investopedia.com/terms/b/bitcoin-w
allet.asp

75. *Investing in Cryptocurrency.* (n.d.-a). Sofi.
https://www.sofi.com/learn/content/investing-in-
cryptocurrency/

76. *Investing in Cryptocurrency.* (n.d.-b). Investor
Junkey.
https://investorjunkie.com/alternative-investmen
ts/investing-in-cryptocurrency/

77. *Investing in Cryptocurrency.* (n.d.-c). Investor
Junkie.
https://investorjunkie.com/alternative-investmen
ts/investing-in-cryptocurrency/

78. J. (2018, July 5). *Introduction to Digital Currency.* Bookdown. https://bookdown.org:443/Jack_Biggs/Cryptocurrency/how-does-cryptocurrency-function.html

79. Kemp, L. (2021, November 30). *Kraken Review.* Coinformant Australia. https://coinformant.com.au/kraken-review/

80. Khojikian, G. (2021, June 17). *The Biggest Risks Of Investing In Bitcoin.* Forbes. https://www.forbes.com/sites/forbesbusinesscouncil/2021/06/17/the-biggest-risks-of-investing-in-bitcoin/?sh=41e4c0bb4afd

81. *Laws & Regulations.* (2019, June 6). Investopedia. https://www.investopedia.com/laws-and-regulations-4427769

82. *List of All Cryptocurrencies | +/-13.000 Coins Listed!* (2021, August 1). Blockspot.Io. https://blockspot.io/coin/

83. *Litecoin (LTC) Price, Charts, and News | Coinbase: litecoin price, litecoin, ltc price.* (2021, November 11). Coinbase. https://www.coinbase.com/price/litecoin

84. *LocalBitcoins.com: Fastest and easiest way to buy and sell bitcoins - LocalBitcoins.* (n.d.). LocalBitcoins. https://localbitcoins.com/

85. M, L. (2021, November 22). *How to Cash Out Bitcoin: How to Do It Easily.* BitDegree.Org Crypto Exchanges. https://www.bitdegree.org/crypto/tutorials/how-to-cash-out-bitcoin

86. Marquit, M. (2021, July 19). *Paper Trading: Experience Investing Without an Actual Risk.*

Investor Junkie.

https://investorjunkie.com/stock-brokers/virtual-trading-account/

87. Marr, B. (2017, December 6). *A Short History Of Bitcoin And Crypto Currency Everyone Should Read.* Forbes.

https://www.forbes.com/sites/bernardmarr/2017/12/06/a-short-history-of-bitcoin-and-crypto-currency-everyone-should-read/?sh=71186cad3f27

88. Messari. (n.d.). *Crypto Research, Data, and Tools.*

https://messari.io/

89. Metrics, C. (2021, July 27). *Network Data Pro.* Coin Metrics.

https://coinmetrics.io/network-data-pro/

90. *Mona.* (n.d.). Mona Co.

https://mona.co/index.html

91. *Money Laundering*. (2021, November 30). Investopedia. https://www.investopedia.com/terms/m/moneyla undering.asp

92. Moskov, A. (2021, November 28). *Stacks (STX) NFTs: Exploring NFTs Secured By Bitcoin.* CoinCentral. https://coincentral.com/what-is-iota-cryptocurre ncy-coin/

93. Munarriz, R. (2021, November 5). *Ethereum Classic - ETC - Stock Price & News*. The Motley Fool. https://www.fool.com/quote/crypto/etc/

94. NordVPN. (2021, November 29). *Nord VPN*. https://go.nordvpn.net/aff_c?offer_id=123&aff_i d=1308&url_id=15076&source=InvestorJunkie& &aff_sub=6b58bf4c366b4ff3aec24211c689afc4

95. Nova, A. (2018, April 10). *How cryptocurrency investors could find themselves behind bars.* CNBC. https://www.cnbc.com/2018/04/09/how-cryptocurrency-investors-could-find-themselves-behind-bars.html

96. *nternal Revenue Service.* (n.d.). IRS. https://www.irs.gov/individuals/international-taxpayers/frequently-asked-questions-on-virtual-currency-transactions

97. Paul, A. (2019, August 10). *Cryptocurrency dealer Pluto Exchange launches India's first bitcoin trading app.* TechGenyz. https://www.techgenyz.com/2017/12/28/pluto-exchange-bitcoin-trading-app-india/

98. *PayPal*. (2021, October 29). Investopedia. https://www.investopedia.com/terms/p/paypal.asp

99. *Peer-to-Peer (P2P) Economy Definition*. (2021, January 1). Investopedia. https://www.investopedia.com/terms/p/peertopeer-p2p-economy.asp

100. *Personal Identification Number (PIN)*. (2020, July 31). Investopedia. https://www.investopedia.com/terms/p/personal-identification-number.asp

101. *The Power of Electronic Money*. (2020, May 31). Investopedia. https://www.investopedia.com/terms/e/electronic-money.asp

102. *Private Key.* (2020, June 29). Investopedia. https://www.investopedia.com/terms/p/private-key.asp

103. *Proof of Stake (PoS).* (2021, April 21). Investopedia. https://www.investopedia.com/terms/p/proof-stake-pos.asp

104. *Proof of Work (PoW).* (2021, July 22). Investopedia. https://www.investopedia.com/terms/p/proof-work.asp

105. Rana, K. (2021, February 21). *Triple entry accounting system: A revolution with blockchain.* Medium. https://medium.com/dataseries/triple-entry-accounting-system-a-revolution-with-blockchain-768f4d8cabd8

106. *Real-time social activity + market metrics for cryptocurrencies | LunarCrush | Coins.* (n.d.). LunarCrush. https://lunarcrush.com/markets?rpp=50

107. *Research Guides: Fintech: Financial Technology Research Guide: Cryptocurrency & Blockchain Technology.* (n.d.). Guides. https://guides.loc.gov/fintech/21st-century/cryptocurrency-blockchain

108. *Risks of using virtual currency | Bitcoin (BTC) Exchange| bitFlyer USA.* (n.d.). Bit Flyer. https://bitflyer.com/en-us/risk

109. *Robinhood.* (n.d.). Investor Junkie. https://investorjunkie.com/wp-json/xm-link/robinhood?p=80716

110. Rosenberg, E. (2021a, April 8). *Dogecoin.* Investor Junkie.

https://investorjunkie.com/crypto/what-is-dogec
oin/

111. Rosenberg, E. (2021b, April 8). *What Is FATCA
and What Does It Mean for Investors?* Investor
Junkie. https://investorjunkie.com/taxes/fatca/

112. Rosic, A., Mitra, R., Mitra, R., Baggetta, M.,
Rosic, A., & Rosic, A. (2020, November 25). *What
is Cryptocurrency? [Everything You Need To
Know!]*. Blockgeeks.
http://blockgeeks.com/guides/what-is-cryptocurr
ency/

113. Rossolillo, N. (2021, September 17). *Types of
Cryptocurrency*. The Motley Fool.
https://www.fool.com/investing/stock-market/m
arket-sectors/financials/cryptocurrency-stocks/ty
pes-of-cryptocurrencies/

114. *Santiment - See what other crypto traders are missing.* (n.d.). Santiment. https://santiment.net/

115. *Seller.* (2021, June 22). Investopedia. https://www.investopedia.com/terms/s/seller.asp

116. *skewAnalytics.* (n.d.). Analytics. https://analytics.skew.com/dashboard/bitcoin-spot

117. *Spice Pay.* (n.d.). Spice Pay. https://spicepay.com/

118. *Stellar - an open network for money.* (n.d.). Stellar. https://www.stellar.org/

119. *Tax Evasion.* (2020, May 29). Investopedia. https://www.investopedia.com/terms/t/taxevasion.asp

120. *Ten Important Cryptocurrencies Other Than Bitcoin.* (2021, December 1). Investopedia.

https://www.investopedia.com/tech/most-import
ant-cryptocurrencies-other-than-bitcoin/

121. *TenX | Official Blog*. (n.d.). TenX.

https://tenx.tech/

122. *Transfer Definition*. (2020, July 30).

Investopedia.

https://www.investopedia.com/terms/t/transfer.a
sp

123. Tretina, K. (2021, July 14). *How To Buy
Cryptocurrency*. Forbes Advisor.

https://www.forbes.com/advisor/investing/how-t
o-buy-cryptocurrency/

124. Trippin', B. B. (2021, May 3). *Why are there so
many cryptocurrencies? What's the point?*
YouTube.

https://www.youtube.com/watch?v=Vr1cIInslRo

125. *Two-Factor Authentication (2FA).* (2020a, September 28). Investopedia. https://www.investopedia.com/terms/t/twofactor-authentication-2fa.asp

126. *Two-Factor Authentication (2FA).* (2020b, September 28). Investopedia. https://www.investopedia.com/terms/t/twofactor-authentication-2fa.asp

127. *Understanding the different types of cryptocurrency.* (n.d.). Sofi. https://www.sofi.com/learn/content/understanding-the-different-types-of-cryptocurrency

128. *Unifimoney.* (n.d.). Investor Junkie. https://investorjunkie.com/wp-json/xm-link/unifimoney?p=80716

129. *Ways to Cash Out Cryptocurrency.* (2021, January 19). Techgenyz.

http://www.techgenyz.com/2021/01/19/ways-to-cash-out-cryptocurrency/

130. *We are DA Hongfei and Erik Zhang founders of NEO the first open source blockchain project from China.* (2017, July 27). Reddit. https://www.reddit.com/r/NEO/comments/6puffo/we_are_da_hongfei_and_erik_zhang_founders_of_neo/

131. *Were There Cryptocurrencies Before Bitcoin?* (2021a, August 26). Investopedia. https://www.investopedia.com/tech/were-there-cryptocurrencies-bitcoin/

132. *Were There Cryptocurrencies Before Bitcoin?* (2021b, August 26). Investopedia. https://www.investopedia.com/tech/were-there-cryptocurrencies-bitcoin/

133. *What are cryptocurrencies?* (n.d.). CMC Markets. https://www.cmcmarkets.com/en/learn-cryptocurrencies/what-are-cryptocurrencies

134. *What Are the Legal Risks to Cryptocurrency Investors?* (2021, October 25). Investopedia. https://www.investopedia.com/tech/what-are-legal-risks-cryptocurrency-investors/

135. *What are the risks?| CMC Markets.* (n.d.). Cmc Markets. https://www.cmcmarkets.com/en/learn-cryptocurrencies/what-are-the-risks

136. *What is a public key?* (2021, June 24). Investopedia. https://www.investopedia.com/terms/p/public-key.asp

137. *What is Bitcoin?* (n.d.). Sofi. https://www.sofi.com/learn/content/what-is-bitcoin/

138. *What Is Blockchain Technology? How Does It Work? | Built In.* (n.d.). Builtin. https://builtin.com/blockchain

139. *What is cryptocurrency?* (n.d.). Coinbase. https://www.coinbase.com/learn/crypto-basics/what-is-cryptocurrency?utm_source=google_search_nb&utm_medium=cpc&utm_campaign=1720998609&utm_content=126549120388&utm_term=cryptocurrencies%20to%20invest%20in&utm_creative=499615487511&cb_device=c&cb_placement=&cb_country=us&cb_city=open&cb_language=en_us&gclid=CjwKCAjw1JeJBhB9EiwAV612yx3pEEyYlUUHL1zZVcO2iesEKMJBub8RcWCmDerjJz8CYuBobKuKvRoC_roQAvD_BwE

140. *What Is Cryptocurrency?* (2021, August 10). Investopedia. https://www.investopedia.com/terms/c/cryptocurrency.asp#:%7E:text=A%20cryptocurrency%20is%20a%20digital,a%20disparate%20network%20of%20computers

141. *What Is Dash Cryptocurrency?* (2021, August 25). Investopedia. https://www.investopedia.com/tech/what-dash-cryptocurrency/

142. *What is Ethereum?* (n.d.). Sofi. https://www.sofi.com/learn/content/what-is-ethereum/

143. *What Is Fiat Money?* (2021, October 26). Investopedia. https://www.investopedia.com/terms/f/fiatmoney.asp#:%7E:text=Fiat%20money%20is%20a%20go

vernment,U.S.%20dollar%2C%20are%20fiat%20c
urrencies

144. *What Is Square, Inc.?* (2021, April 15). Investopedia. https://www.investopedia.com/articles/tech/0210 17/square.asp

145. *What Is ZCash?* (2020, April 30). Investopedia. https://www.investopedia.com/terms/z/zcash.asp

146. *Who Is Satoshi Nakamoto?* (2021, July 21). Investopedia. https://www.investopedia.com/terms/s/satoshi-n akamoto.asp

147. *Why do we have different cryptocurrencies?* (n.d.). Quora. https://www.quora.com/Why-do-we-have-differe nt-cryptocurrencies

148. *Wire Transfer Definition.* (2021, August 17).

Investopedia.

https://www.investopedia.com/terms/w/wiretran

sfer.asp

149. Wong, J. I. (2018, May 22). *Bitcoin Pizza Day 2018: Eight years ago, someone bought two pizzas with bitcoins now worth $82 million.* Quartz.

https://qz.com/1285209/bitcoin-pizza-day-2018-eight-years-ago-someone-bought-two-pizzas-with-bitcoins-now-worth-82-million/

Made in the USA
Middletown, DE
14 February 2022